Dynamic Dating: ♥

We speak all over the country on love, sex, and dating. And everywhere we go students ask us the same questions again and again.

When should I start dating?

How do I decide who to date?

Should I date a non-Christian?

How can I be more appealing to the opposite sex?

How can I get a date?

What are some different ideas of things to do on dates?

What should I do if I'm not dating?

How can I get a date to go out with me more than once?

When should I go with just one person?

How can I break up without someone getting hurt?

How can I set standards in my dating?

Wouldn't it be nice if someone had devised a formula for dynamic dating? Well, no one has developed such a formula. But someone has laid down principles that will guide you into dynamic dating relationships. We know — from personal experience and from our talks with thousands of young men and women — that these principles work.

The purpose of this book is to answer your questions about dating and to give you practical steps for dynamic dating based on those principles.

DATING

Picking (and Being) a Winner

Barry St. Clair & Bill Jones

Here's Life Publishers

Published by
HERE'S LIFE PUBLISHERS, INC.
P. O. Box 1576
San Bernardino, CA 92402

HLP Product No. 951707

Printed in the United States of America.

Library of Congress Cataloging-in-Publication Data
St. Clair, Barry.
      Dating : picking (and being) a winner.
      Bibliography: p.
      Summary: A handbook for dating, discussing such areas as getting dates,
keeping dates, dating creatively, going steady, breaking up, and setting standards.
Provides a Christian viewpoint.
      1. Dating (Social customs) — Juvenile literature. 2. Interpersonal rela-
tions — Juvenile literature. 3. Dating (Social customs) — Religious aspects — Chris-
tianity — Juvenile literature. [1. Dating (Social customs) 2. Christian life]
I. Jones, Bill, 1955-
II. Title.
HQ801.S75   1987   646.7'7   87-62
ISBN 0-89840-172-0 (pbk.)

Unless otherwise indicated, Scripture quotations are from *The New
American Standard Bible,* ©The Lockman Foundation 1960, 1962,
1963, 1968, 1971, 1972, 1975, 1977.

Scripture quotations designated (NIV) are from *The Holy Bible, New
International Version,* ©1978 by New York International Bible Society,
published by the Zondervan Corporation, Grand Rapids, Michigan.

FOR MORE INFORMATION, WRITE:

L.I.F.E. — P.O. Box A399, Sydney South 2000, Australia
Campus Crusade for Christ of Canada — Box 300, Vancouver, B.C., V6C 2X3, Canada
Campus Crusade for Christ — Pearl Assurance House, 4 Temple Row, Birmingham, B2 5HG, England
Campus Crusade for Christ — P.O. Box 240, Colombo Court Post Office, Singapore 9117
Lay Institute for Evangelism — P.O. Box 8786, Auckland 3, New Zealand
Great Commission Movement of Nigeria — P.O. Box 500, Jos, Plateau State Nigeria, West Africa
Campus Crusade for Christ International — Arrowhead Springs, San Bernardino, CA 92414, U.S.A.

FIRST PRINTING, JULY 1987
SECOND PRINTING, AUGUST 1987
THIRD PRINTING, SEPTEMBER 1987
FOURTH PRINTING, NOVEMBER 1987
FIFTH PRINTING, FEBRUARY 1988
SIXTH PRINTING, JUNE 1988

To our wives,
Carol and Debby,
who are all-time winners.

Special Thanks

To Richard and Diane Welch, whose sacrifice enabled us to write this book.

To Gina Dixon, for learning to read our handwriting and faithfully typing the manuscript.

To Chris Frear, for his editing and creative input.

To all the students and youth workers who have attended our Breakaway Conferences and have proved the benefits of the principles in this book.

To our families, who have encouraged us in the writing of this book.

Contents

You Are Important!

Are you worried about dating? Are you frustrated?

If you're like the average teen, then you probably are. But relax — let Barry St. Clair and Bill Jones help you out.

It's been my privilege, as Series Editor, to work with these two gifted men. These guys know young people. They each have years of experience working with students, like yourself. Through their work with Reach Out Ministries they've hosted numerous dating seminars across the country, keeping them in contact with today's young people and the questions they're asking: from the very basic "Where do I start?" to the more complicated "How do we know when we're ready for commitment?" or "We've just broken up — now what?" Sound familiar?

Barry and Bill offer *practical* advice for fun, Christ-centered dating. They provide tips on how to maximize your dating potential, lists of ideas to get you out of the dating rut, and guidelines to help you tell a winner from a loser . . . and that's just the beginning. Step by step, they will help you work through the confusion and develop a dating life that not only satisfies you but honors God as well.

You are important. God cares about your dating life. It's my prayer that this book will guide you in your commitment to God as you learn to trust *every* area of your life to Him.

Josh McDowell
Series Editor

Introduction

One of the drawbacks of being young is a tendency to not think about how present choices will affect your whole life. This is true in every area of life, but the effects show up the most in love, sex and dating. We know; we have experienced it — both the negative and positive. Our desire in writing this book is that, as you learn and apply these ideas and principles, you will not only pick a winner, but that you also will *be* the winner that you were meant to be.

Barry St. Clair & Bill Jones
Reach Out Ministries
120 N. Avondale Road
Avondale Estates, GA 30002

1

Understanding Dating ♥

*D*ATING is fun. Few things can get people as fired up as dating. Once you have a date you think about it for days. You anticipate every minute of it. You get ready for hours, making sure everything is perfect. Then you go out to a fun place with a person you like and spend hours together. Dating is definitely fun.

Dating is also confusing. With all the dates and all the people who have dated over the years, you would think everyone would understand more about it. It seems like you should know how to date a guy or girl without running into so many problems. But no one has put all the knowledge about dating into one place, so it seems every young man and woman has to go through the same things personally.

Dan's experience sums all this up. Being a bright guy, he figured that before he started dating he'd do a little research. But there was nothing in the encyclopedia, and the dictionary wasn't much help. When he looked up "dates" at the library, he found a couple of great books — about how to make date fruit bread. But nothing on dating. Now he's really mixed up.

Dating puts people into situations where they don't know what they should do. For example, how would you respond in the following situations?

DATING QUIZ[1]

1. Your date has super bad breath. You should:

_____ A. Wear a pained expression and wave your hand in front of your nose.

_____ B. Tell about your Uncle Milton whose false teeth need to be cleaned because they smell.

_____ C. Pretend you don't notice and enjoy yourself anyway.

_____ D. Explain that your parents won't let you stay out on a date for more than fifteen minutes.

2. You have just finished eating a seven-course meal at an expensive restaurant when your date whispers that he has left his wallet in another pair of pants. You should:

_____ A. Swoon in a dead faint.

_____ B. Accuse him of knowingly tricking you and kick him under the table.

_____ C. Loan him a quarter to call home.

_____ D. Let him use your college savings to pay the bill.

3. You're dating for the first time after breaking up with your steady. You see your old steady at the pizza place as you walk in. You should:

_____ A. Grab your date's arm and put your nose in the air.

_____ B. Sashay by your old steady's table while remarking, "I used to date that creepy person. I'm glad it's over."

_____ C. Simulate a violent heart attack.

_____ D. Act as normal as possible.

4. You're at a party and the hostess has run out of cups. You

should:
_____ A. Dip your friend's cup into the punch while you joke, "We all have the same germs anyway."
_____ B. Burst into tears and make a scene.
_____ C. Sprinkle cornflakes on her velvet chairs.
_____ D. Smile and say that you would be glad to wash some cups if that would help.

5. Your parents have informed you that you cannot use the car for your date this weekend. You should:
_____ A. Remind them that they dedicated you to God and ask them, "What would God do in your place?"
_____ B. Laugh hysterically.
_____ C. Make arrangements to double date.
_____ D. Sew your father's pajama legs together.

6. Before the annual sweetheart banquet, your face breaks out like a studded tire. You should:
_____ A. Forget your face and have a ball.
_____ B. Lie under a sun lamp for three hours so no one will know the difference.
_____ C. Tell everyone you know that you had a run-in with the neighbor's cat.
_____ D. Call your date and explain that you have leprosy.

7. You are going out with the one person you've longed to date. It's suddenly mentioned that everyone who's anyone ends a date at Lover's Lookout. You should:
_____ A. Do what comes naturally.
_____ B. Suggest another way to end your date.
_____ C. Sob uncontrollably for forty-five minutes.
_____ D. Recite the Lord's Prayer.

8. You're on a double date and would much rather be with your friend's date than your own date. You should:

_____ A. Pout all night and make everyone miserable.
_____ B. Tell your own date that your friend is more witty and charming than you are.
_____ C. Make the best of it and try again next time.
_____ D. Talk loudly about the new trend in date-swapping.

9. Your parents are waiting up for you with that "you'd-better-have-a-good-reason" look on their faces when you come in late from your date. You should:
_____ A. Smirk knowingly and let them think the worst.
_____ B. Explain that the police kept you for questioning after the jewelry store was bombed.
_____ C. Apologize and try to be more prompt next time.
_____ D. Suggest a midnight snack.
(Answers on page 24)

In dating, you will encounter awkward situations like these. The answers to these are fairly obvious, but how many times have you had a question about dating and not known what to do or who to ask?

We speak all over the country on love, sex, and dating every year. And everywhere we go students ask us the same basic questions again and again.

What is dating?
When should I start dating?
How do I decide who to date?
Should I date a non-Christian?
How can I get a date?
What are some different ideas to do on dates?
What should I do if I'm not dating?
How can I get a date to go out with me more than once?
When should I go with just one person?
How can I break up without someone getting hurt?
How can I set standards in my dating?

Wouldn't it be nice if someone had devised a formula for dynamic dating? Wouldn't it make things easier to simply follow a five-step formula and — *Bing!* — out pops a wonderful relationship?

Well, no one has developed such a formula and no one ever will, because dating involves people and people are unpredictable and don't fit into formulas. That's the bad news.

But someone has laid down principles that will guide you into dynamic dating relationships. He's internationally known and respected. A man whose teaching is the most repeated and distributed in the world. He knows young people better than anyone. He knows the best solution for every situation. He knows all the joys and embarrassments of life and dating.

That person is Jesus Christ, and He has written His principles for dating in His Word — the Bible.

The purpose of this book is to answer your questions about dating and to give you practical steps for dynamic dating based on the principles Jesus provides in the Bible.

How do we, as the authors, know these principles will guide you to dynamic dating? Because both of us have dated with and without these principles and have talked with thousands of students who have done the same. Over and over we found that Jesus understands dating and has a complete dating plan for you. With that in mind, let's tackle the first question, "What is dating?"

THE SET-UP

Dating is not universal. In many societies, until this century parents prearranged marriages, and even in many countries today that is still the custom.

Imagine how that would go over today. Your parents and the next door neighbors are best friends. One night they discuss how much you kids enjoy each other. One thing leads to another, and before the night is over a formal arrangement has been made: At eighteen years of age, the two of you will be married.

It doesn't bother you at first, because all two-year-olds look and act the same, but by second grade you begin to wonder if your parents did you right. Every day after lunch your "fiancé" wets his pants. By junior high he is a foot shorter than you and has never washed his hair. By high school he dresses like a nerd and embarrasses you by eating with his hands. To make matters worse, because you are "engaged," you are not allowed to go out with anyone else. What a nightmare!

Can you believe that is how it was done?

Look around you; dating has taken America by storm. Just the mention of the word gets everyone's attention. It seems that everyone who is eligible to date is either waiting to, wanting to, or actually dating.

DIFFERENT STYLES

Dating has developed into many different styles. Each style has people who have their own characteristics and problems. As you read, think about people you know who fit these styles. Think too, about what you like and don't like about each style as you see it in people's lives. What can you learn from them to develop a healthier and more fun dating life?[2]

Dreamers think about dating all week. They daydream about who they would enjoy dating the most, how they will get together, where they will go, what they will do, how the relationship will develop, how they might even get married. But weeks come and go and they don't act on their dreams.

Jeff and Rachel have a great relationship — in Jeff's mind. He's never talked to her, but he thinks about her all day long. He chooses his classes by which ones she'll be in. And he always grabs the seat two rows behind her and one over, so he can look at her the whole period. He's even figured out when they'll go on their honeymoon — if he could ever ask her out.

Fanatics date and date and date. All they ever do is

date. Their whole life is centered around dating. They fear that if they go one day without a date, they will die (or at least fall into a coma). The fanatic feels like something must be wrong if he or she doesn't have someone to date.

The football team may be 9-0, but Emily has the longest streak in school history. She has gone out every Friday and Saturday night since third grade. She's never *heard* of "Friday Night Videos."

Scooters are "madly in love" with one person one day and with another person the next. The scooters rush blindly into relationship after relationship. Love to them is an emotional high. When they come down, they quickly look around for another person to date.

Jamie has a policy — never wear the same dress with the same guy twice. And since she has only two dresses, she has to keep moving. She's glad she'll graduate this year, because there are only seventy-four guys left in the school who she hasn't dated.

Lifers have gone together since kindergarten. From the first they knew they had found the right one. Their motto is "till death do us part." They are in the minority, but most schools have at least one or two couples who adhere to this approach (and to each other).

Sometimes they wonder if they have made the right choice, but they worry more about not finding anyone else. So, they hang together on their life-long journey.

Rick can still remember his and Leann's first date: They crawled to the television to watch Sesame Street. In fact, every year to commemorate that date, they sit down and watch it again. This year will make sixteen straight years.

Clingers take the physical approach. They hang all over each other. They gross everyone out by making out between classes. To the clingers the most important aspect of a relationship is the physical.

Greg is ecstatic. He has finally figured out how to have some privacy with his new girlfriend between classes. He rigged his locker so they can climb inside, lock the door and still get out. He's especially happy, because he tried it once before and he and Brenda got stuck in the locker for four days. (She broke up with him when they got out.)

Fighters fuss and feud. These couples are like two cats with their tails tied together. They have unity — they can't give each other up — but they don't have any peace. When they break up, they make up before the next weekend.

There's a betting scandal at Matt and Wendy's school. One of the students is setting odds every week on how soon the two will go on their first date after they break up. He's figured out that they usually break up Saturday night and go out again Monday.

These styles include most of the students' dating. Each one has good and bad aspects. For example, the fighters are quick to get over their problems. Clingers either have to be creative to think up ways to make out privately, or they have to be bold enough to make out in front of everyone. However, the true motive behind all of these styles of dating is selfishness:

- To satisfy my ego.
- To look good in other people's eyes.
- To satisfy my physical desires.
- To keep from being lonely.
- To keep from being bored.
- To feel loved.
- To be popular.
- To get someone else jealous.
- To please my friends.
- To be like everyone else.
- To find a marriage partner.

With so many different styles of dating, and problems and benefits with each one, no wonder people are so confused.

THE ALTERNATIVE

You're probably thinking, "Great! Now you've got me even more confused." But there are answers. To help you work through the confusion, it is helpful to see what Jesus has to say. Let's face it, He created you to live in relationships and He knows what works and what doesn't.

Although the Bible doesn't refer specifically to dating, it does contain clear direction on relationships. As you learn God's Word, you will discover an obvious difference between the styles of dating you normally see at school and God's style of dating.

God loves you and has your best interests at heart, from your home life to your school life and even your dating life. Because of His love for you, Jesus Christ wants to be right at the center of your dating relationships. He wants to be the focal point of all that you do and to give your life meaning and direction.

And in Ephesians 4:1-3 the apostle Paul tells you how to do that:

> I, therefore, the prisoner of the Lord, entreat you to walk in a manner worthy of the calling with which you have been called, with all humility and gentleness, with patience, showing forbearance to one another in love, being diligent to preserve the unity of the Spirit in the bond of peace.

These three verses present three solid ways that you can practice God's style of dating, which leads to a lot less confusion and a whole lot more fun.

Honor Jesus Christ

Ephesians 4:1 says to "walk in a manner worthy of the calling. . ." A Christian's calling is to be a worthy follower of Jesus Christ. Since He deserves no less than the best from you, *everything* in your dating should honor Him. That's not easy — to surrender every last detail and action to Christ — but here's how you can learn to "walk worthy of Christ" in your dating.

● *Purify your motives.* Most styles of dating don't work because they are based at least partly on selfishness. But following God's style of dating emphasizes a whole different set of motives for dating. In God's style of dating, you:

— Date to become a better *person.* When you build relationships with others through dating, you mature; you grow spiritually, mentally, emotionally, and socially.

— Date to become a better *friend.* In your dating you want to consider your date's needs first. The more you serve him or her, the more you grow in your friendship. You also communicate. This helps you get to know each other better and work through any trouble spots.

— Date to become a better *partner.* Spending time with your date helps you understand the numerous ways a guy or girl is different from you. You learn to communicate openly and honestly. You learn to relax and enjoy being around him. Every experience helps prepare you for your future marriage partner.

Every time you discover a selfish desire in your dating, turn it over to Jesus Christ. Ask Him to take it away. Never allow your own selfish desires to motivate you.

● *Change your actions.* Your motives for dating will determine the way you act on dates. For example, if you date to satisfy your sexual desires, you will be overly involved physically. Likewise, if you date to build friendships, you will let the relationship develop slowly and never pressure the other person to be more serious.

If you have wrong motives, changing your reason for dating will not by itself automatically change the habits you have developed from the past. Therefore, you'll have to work on changing your actions to build new habits.

Think about your behavior on dates. Does your dating honor Jesus? Is there anything about your dating that doesn't honor Him?

If someone were to print what you did on your last date in the school newspaper, would it shame or honor —
yourself?
your date?
your parents?
your Lord?

When you discover any problem areas, make the necessary changes.

Put Others First

Ephesians 4:2 says to be humble, gentle, patient, forbearing, and loving toward one another. This cannot happen if you focus on yourself. But when you concentrate on these attitudes, you will be able to put the needs of others ahead of your own. When you do this, not only will your attitude change, but your date's attitude will also change. Your service will motivate him or her to be more giving and considerate.

● *Humility.* When you are humble you consider the other person as more important than yourself. When you have this attitude, you want to meet any need your date has. You will find yourself thinking of your date's needs before your own. Humility does *not* mean that you think you're a slug, but it does mean you count your date as very valuable.

● *Gentleness.* When you are gentle, you carefully avoid hurting your date's feelings. Instead, you sensitively build up that person with kind words, avoiding harsh words. This is just as important for guys as for girls.

● *Patience.* No two people are exactly alike in needs, desires and attitudes. If you concentrate on your own wants in a relationship, you will become irritated with the other person. A patient person, however, recognizes the differences in others and allows them room to grow at their own pace. You need to wait for the other person as he or she grows.

● *Forbearance.* Putting others ahead of yourself is not always easy. As you learn to serve, even your date may mistreat you — intentionally or by accident. Forbearance is enduring any suffering the other may cause.

● *Love.* This isn't the emotion-filled, possessive, shallow love that is found in the other styles of dating. When you love others, you want them to have God's best. You aren't satisfied until they receive all that Christ wants to give them.

Develop Close Friendships

After many couples have been dating for a while they begin to get on each other's nerves. They focus on the little points of friction rather than on the major positive points that brought them together. When this type of couple breaks up, they rarely feel as close to each other again, because of all the guilt and hurt feelings.

But it can be much different. God's style of dating results in continued friendships. God's Word instructs you to seek diligently to keep "unity and peace" in your relationships (Ephesians 4:3). But how do you do that?

● *Recognize that disagreements will occur.* No two people ever agree on everything every time. Have you and your best friend always agreed on everything? Of course not, so don't expect to always agree with anyone else.

● *Realize that you must make choices.* When disagreements arise, you can either push away or pull together. Considering the other's needs and point of view are keys to pulling together. Even if you both recognize that it's best to break up, you can still pull together in friendship.

● *Respond to differences by communicating.* Talk things out. Admit when you are wrong and the other person is right, but when there is no "right" answer, try to reach a compromise. Be quick to ask forgiveness and to forgive. Don't always demand or expect your own way.

Working through differences makes stronger, closer friendships.

A DEFINITION

That's a lot to consider. How can we condense all that

we just covered into a simple statement? See how this works. God's style of dating is:

A growing friendship between a guy and a girl which honors Jesus Christ as each person puts the other's needs first.

When Christ is central in your life, He will be central in your dating. When He is, you will be motivated to consider your date's needs above your own as you seek God's will together. The definition above does not limit you to dating only one person. Nor does it say that you have to be "in love" to date. That should take some pressure off you, and help you to better understand dating.

ACTION SECTION

1. What style of dating (Dreamers, Fanatics, Scooters, Lifers, Clingers, Fighters) characterizes most of your dating in the past?

_____

2. What have been your reasons for dating? _____
_____

How do you feel about those reasons in light of Ephesians 4:1-3? _____
_____
_____

3. Write down the main area in your dating that you need to work on to bring honor to Jesus Christ.

_____

Name three steps you will take to do this.
(1) _____
(2) _____
(3) _____

4. Which attitude in Ephesians 4:2 do you need to work on the most?

What steps will you take to do this?
(1) _____
(2) _____
(3) _____

5. List three steps to take to handle differences in your relationships.
(1) _____
(2) _____
(3) _____

6. Memorize Ephesians 4:1

Answers to Quiz:
1-C   4-D   7-B
2-C   5-C   8-C
3-D   6-A   9-C

Number right:
8-9 sharp
6-7 not as sharp
4-5 need time on the grindstone
1-3 get a new blade

2

Starting Right ♥

TEENAGERS fight more battles with parents over dating than just about any other issue. And a lot of the conflicts center on when to start dating. Most teens know they're old enough — you probably do, too — but most parents were born in the Dark Ages. They think you'll never be ready. So they confine you to endless weeks of dateless weekends.

HOW OLD IS OLD ENOUGH?

The main problem is that you and your folks are looking at the situation from different perspectives — neither of you is measuring your dating age by the same scale. They're looking backward from years of experience and looking mostly at the problems. But you're looking ahead toward all the fun you imagine you'll have.

To see clearly where you and your parents stand, make an "X" by the right answer in the quiz below, then make a "*" by what your parents would say as to when you're ready to date.

A. Born ready to date.   _____
B. Six.   _____
C. Twelve.   _____
D. Sixteen.   _____
E. Eighteen.   _____
F. Twenty-one or older.   _____
G. Not until you're married.   _____
H. None of the above.   _____

Anyone in his right mind knows you were born ready to date. Right?

Wrong!

It sounds right, but there can be serious consequences to dating before you're ready. For example, one young girl liked a guy at school, but she knew he had some bad habits. She knew she shouldn't date him until he straightened those out. Finally, she gave in and dated him under the pretense that he would "settle down." Naively, she believed him. And kept on believing him until they got married. She was counseled to wait, but she answered, "We're in love. It will work out."

Only one month after their wedding, he resumed his old habits. But she stayed with him, hoping that he would hold to his promise and change. Then one day, to her amazement, he told her he was tired of being "tied down." He wanted his freedom.

Abruptly, divorce erased five years of marriage. She found herself responsible for two young children. Having only a high school education, she couldn't find a job to provide for them adequately.

This girl was living in an unfortunate present facing an uncertain future because of an irresponsible past.

She experienced the full force of The Law of the Harvest:

You reap what you sow.

You reap more than you sow.
You reap later than you sow.

She sowed an immature decision. Later, she reaped many results of that decision.

Many dating problems, as well as many marriage problems, result from one or both of the individuals starting to date before he or she is old enough. Consider this research: 91 percent of girls who began dating at age twelve had sex before graduation, compared with 56 percent who had dated at thirteen; 53 percent who dated at fourteen; 40 percent who dated at fifteen; *and 20 percent who dated at sixteen.* Seventy percent of boys with a ninth-grade steady said they'd had sex, compared to 60 percent of girls; 52 percent of boys who dated occasionally as freshmen had sex, compared to 35 percent of girls.

The girl in the previous example was definitely not old enough to date, because she did not have the maturity to resist her emotions and make a responsible choice.

The real answer to the right age to start dating is "H" — "none of the above." Being old enough to date is not a physical age. Instead, it is an issue of maturity: spiritual, emotional and social maturity. It shows up in the quality of your relationship with your parents and especially in your ability to resist physical involvement consistently and completely. The statistics quoted earlier show that most students start dating long before they are ready.

HOW TO GROW OLD ENOUGH

"That's great," you say, "but that doesn't help me show my parents I'm old enough." That's the whole purpose of this next section — to give you a practical measuring stick for your maturity. In the New Testament, 1 Timothy 4:12 provides some good, general guidelines to start you off:

Let no one look down on your youthfulness, but rather in speech, conduct, love, faith, and purity, show yourself an example of those who believe.

You are old enough to date when you are an example of what a Christian really is. Someone old enough to date is committed daily to speech, conduct, love, faith and purity that glorify the Lord Jesus. That is maturity in all its forms.

To get specific, let's look at each of these areas individually.

Speech

This doesn't mean those five-minute talks you have to give in front of your English class. It's what you say every day in normal conversation.

When you're mature enough to date, your speech is under the control of Jesus Christ. In his letter to the Christians in Ephesus, Paul tells them how to do this:

> Do not let any unwholesome talk come out of your mouths, but only what is helpful for building others up according to their needs, that it may benefit those who listen (Ephesians 4:29).

In "building others up," your speech is filled with praise and thanksgiving to God. You praise Him for who He is and thank Him for what He has done. Also, you compliment and encourage others. Your praise and encouragement is specific and sincere.

When you "avoid" ungodly talk, your speech does not include cursing, gossiping, lying, or putting down others. If you can't yet control your tongue, you're not mature enough to date.

When your speech is filled with the positive and contains none of the negative, that's the first sign you're ready to begin dating.

For example, what would you say if one afternoon after school, you walked to your new car and found a dent in the door? Or you found the inside of your car was soaked by rain because your little brother left the window down? What words would come out of your mouth then?

On a scale of one to ten, how would you rate your speech according to Ephesians 4:29?

1   2   3   4   5   6   7   8   9   10
Needs   Doing
work   great

Conduct

A second measure of your maturity is whether your conduct — actions — consistently reflects Christ's conduct as found in the Bible. This doesn't mean you have to be perfect. It does mean, though, that you are striving for the best, constantly trying to do what's right. If you blow it — that is, if your actions hurt either God or another person — then it means you go back and ask both God and that person to forgive you. The apostle Paul wrote in Acts 24:16: "In view of this, I also do my best to maintain always a blameless conscience both before God and before men." Think of your own life. Is there an issue that you haven't resolved yet? If there is, pay attention to the chart coming up.

Having a clear conscience is important for many reasons other than just being old enough to date. Without a clear conscience:

- You cannot enjoy fellowship with God (Isaiah 59:1,2).
- You lose your joy (Psalm 33:3-5).
- You find your Christian life going to pieces (1 Timothy 1:18,19).
- You are not as close to the person you hurt (Matthew 5:23,24).
- You will give non-Christians a reason to discredit your testimony for Christ (1 Peter 3:16).

If any of these sound familiar, ask God to remind you of anyone you have offended. It may be Himself, your parents, brothers or sisters, friends, former friends, teachers, or employers. When you remember someone, write down who it was and what you did. Next, write what you need to do to ask forgiveness. For example, if you stole something, you need to ask forgiveness and then replace it or pay for it. That's called restitution.

Here's a helpful chart to fill out when you pray about this:

Who I offended	The offense	What I need to do	When accomplished
Mr. Ollman	Wrote extra hours on my time card at work.	(1) Ask God to forgive me. (2) Ask Mr. Ollman to forgive me. (3) Pay back those hours.	Friday 3/12

When you go to ask forgiveness, there are three things you should say. First, tell the person that your conduct was wrong. Then, let him know how sorry you are for what you did. Last, ask forgiveness. These three things — "I was wrong," "I am sorry," and "Will you please forgive me?" — cover all you need to say to clear your conscience.

Never put this off. You can think of all kinds of excuses not to follow through, but if you're preparing yourself to date, you must have a clear conscience.

Love

Love is not a fuzzy-wuzzy, romantic kind of feeling, but a commitment to giving another person God's very best.

1 Corinthians 13:4-8 talks about this kind of love. Below are the characteristics found in the verses. Read the passage first, then the definition for each characteristic, and finally rate yourself on each one.

Characteristic	Definition	Bad	Needs work	Okay	Great
Patient	calmly enduring problems	_____	_____	_____	_____
Kind	considering others first	_____	_____	_____	_____
Not jealous	not upset when date gives attention to others	_____	_____	_____	_____
Doesn't brag	doesn't try to impress others	_____	_____	_____	_____
Not arrogant	not conceited, cocky	_____	_____	_____	_____
Doesn't act unbecomingly	not rude or disrespectful	_____	_____	_____	_____
Doesn't seek its own	not selfish	_____	_____	_____	_____
Not provoked	doesn't get angry or lose one's temper	_____	_____	_____	_____
Doesn't take into account a wrong suffered	not resentful, forgives easily and sincerely	_____	_____	_____	_____
Doesn't rejoice in un-righteousness	doesn't have fun doing wrong	_____	_____	_____	_____
Rejoices in truth	has fun doing right	_____	_____	_____	_____
Bears all things	supportive, encouraging during troubles	_____	_____	_____	_____

Characteristic	Definition	Bad	Needs work	Okay	Great
Believes all things	trusting, thinks the best of others	____	____	____	____
Hopes all things	confident that things will get better	____	____	____	____
Endures all things	hangs tough during difficult times	____	____	____	____
Never fails	dependable	____	____	____	____

How did you do? If all your answers were in the two right-hand columns, you are definitely learning how to love. And that is another step in being ready to date. If not, work on these areas with the help of the action section at the end of this chapter.

Faith

The main way a student demonstrates how much he trusts God (faith) is obeying what his parents say about his dating. No joke. Obviously, this is hard at times, because you may think your parents do not understand, which may or may not be true. However, if God is in control of the universe, then surely He is in control of your parents. Any time He wants to, God can change your parents' hearts and minds (check out Proverbs 21:1).

In most cases, parents want only what they think is best for you. God very often uses parents and others in authority to protect you from harm and guide you in the right direction. By trusting God to work through your parents, you show faith.

For example, your parents may not want you to date a specific person you are just dying to go out with. Here is where faith comes into action. This happened to two friends of ours. Instead of pouting, refusing to speak to their parents, or threatening to run away, they chose to obey joyfully. Several months later, after they had demonstrated the maturity to wait, the parents knew they could be trusted. At that point the parents gave them permission to date. Was it easy for them to wait? Of course not! But it was worth it, because they grew from the experience and their parents held real trust for them and the maturity they showed.

You need to remember:

(1) God loves you enough to want the best for you,

(2) He is wise enough to know what's best for you, and

(3) He is powerful enough to get the best for you.

So by faith you can trust God to work through your parents, whether they are Christians or not.

You're ready to date when you choose to obey your parents as proof of your faith in God.

Purity

You are mature enough to date when you not only have made up your mind not to compromise physically, but also have the ability to follow through on this commitment to purity.

God's purpose for your dating is to grow in friendship, remember? He wants you to wait until marriage before getting involved physically. He desires this because He knows the potential consequences if you don't. Here are just a few: loss of virginity, an unwanted pregnancy, an illegitimate child, guilt from abortion, venereal disease, a forced marriage, shame, guilt, flashbacks, loss of reputation, and loss of self-respect.

Now look at the consequences if you do obey God's desire: Purity. No guilt. Extra-special wedding night. Protection from venereal diseases. Children as God plans and desires. Enhanced testimony of your life. Not only must you decide not to compromise in your physical relationships in the future, but also you must have a clear conscience about all of your dating relationships in the past.

Let's get specific on what "involvement," "compromise," and "too far" mean. Buckle your seatbelt: intercourse of any type; fondling genitals or breasts either with or without clothes on; simulating intercourse with clothes on; or caressing the body.

If this happened in any relationship you've been in, how can you get a clear conscience?

1. Admit to God that what you did was wrong.
2. Receive His forgiveness, knowing that He forgets sin as soon as He forgives.
3. Talk to the other person and ask his or her forgiveness.

When you have made the decision not to compromise physically and have the commitment to follow through, and have cleared your conscience from anything in the past, this is a good indication that you are ready to date.

TEST TIME

At the beginning of this chapter you may have thought you were ready to date, but now you see how maturity really determines if you're ready. Test your maturity with the questions below.

1. **Speech.**   Enter your speech rating from page 31.   ____
2. **Conduct.**   Check all the statements that are true about
        you:
My conduct is more and more Christ-like.
                                (15 points)   ____
I filled out the chart on getting a blameless conscience and have gone to everyone on the chart
to clear my conscience.   (20 points)   ____
                        Enter #2 total here.____
3. **Love.**   Turn back to the section on love.
        Give yourself:
        −2 points every time you checked *Bad*.
        −1 point every time you checked *Needs work*.
        +1 point every time you checked *Okay*.
        +2 points every time you checked *Great*.
                        Enter #3 total here.____
4. **Faith.**   Ask your parents if they think you're
        honoring them in your dating.

Yes (24 points)   ____
No (0 points)   ____

5. **Purity.**   Do you have a clear conscience with
everyone of the opposite sex?
Yes (12 points)   ____
No (0 points)   ____
Are you committed to staying pure?
Yes (12 points)   ____
No (0 points)   ____
Add up your TOTAL POINTS. Enter here.   ____

Check where you are on the following grading scale.

____   0-20   points — Get off the streets! See your pastor
immediately!

____   21-40 points — You can stay on the streets — or at
least until dark — but your youth
minister can help you a lot!

____   41-60 points — Definitely not ready to date, but you
have hope if you keep on working.

____   61-80 points — You're almost there. Strengthen your
weak areas, then check again.

____   81-100 points — GREAT! You show signs of being
"old enough" to date. Talk with your
parents — show them this test —
and pay close attention to the chapter
on getting dates.

____   101-125 points — TREMENDOUS! Keep doing what
you are doing!

ACTION SECTION

1. If you score under 80 points, go back and work on the test
until you do better. What was your score on:
1. Speech   ____   out of 10 points
2. Conduct   ____   out of 35 points
3. Love   ____   out of 32 points

    4. Faith   ____   out of 24 points
    5. Purity   ____   out of 24 points

In what area can you gain the most points if you work on that area?

_____

What one practical project can you do this week to improve that area?

_____

_____

What are some long-term projects you can do to improve that area and keep it consistent? _____

_____

_____

_____

2. Memorize 1 Timothy 4:12

3

Picking Winners ♥

EVERYONE has a mental picture of Mr. or Miss Right. Maybe you even have a poster of him or her on your wall. You probably know exactly what you want your perfect date to look and act like. So when a prospect comes along, you immediately measure him or her against your mental picture.

Ways of evaluating the perfect date often fall into three general categories — the Big Three — looks, personality and popularity. Every person is unique, so there are as many different possibilities within each of these categories as there are people.

LOOKS

Under looks, there are three main considerations: size, shape and color.

Size. This makes life difficult, because tall people feel too tall, short people feel too short, and everyone else wants to be either taller or shorter.

As for dates, generally girls don't care nearly as much as guys do — as long as she's not 6'4" and he's 5'2". Guys don't care either — as long as the girl is the same height or shorter than he is. Guys tend to have problems dating girls taller than they are, probably because they fear cutting remarks from self-appointed wise guys. It's bad enough being shorter than everyone else on the basketball team. But shorter than your date, too?

Shape. Shape means the space the person's body occupies. Some dates are lightweights and take up as much space as a salt shaker. (They're the ones who can eat forever and not put on a pound, too.) Others are heavyweights and take up more space than a salt shaker, a chair and the dining room table. But most dates are somewhere in between. The most important thing to people is how the weight is proportioned to the person's body. Someone 150 pounds and 5'10" probably looks OK, but 450 pounds on a person three feet tall might not.

Color. Different people have different colors. People range from fair to dark complexion, with all shades in between. Along with different skin tones come hair color and eye color. Some dates have blonde hair, some brown, some black, some red. And some have no hair at all. Eye color is the same — some have blue, brown, green.

PERSONALITY

Again, personalities are unique, so they differ with each person. However, people usually fall into one of these four types, or a combination of them.[1]

"Larry and Laurie Life-Of-The-Party." Larry and Laurie are extremely outgoing, non-stop talkers and great storytellers. They make you laugh, and are fun to be with, because they are happy, optimistic, and enthusiastic. Larry and Laurie like people and make friends easily, but they hate to be alone. At the end of the year, Larry and Laurie are voted "Class Clown," "Most Talkative," and "Most Popular."

"Allen and Amy Achiever." Allen and Amy are outgoing,

too. But while Larry and Laurie are talkers, Allen and Amy are doers. They were born to lead. They exude confidence, and are dynamic and active. Rarely are they discouraged. Since Allen and Amy make decisions easily, they take charge when they show up. That's one reason they're often elected as presidents and captains of different clubs and sports teams.

"Sam and Susie Serious." Sam and Susie look serious a lot, because they're always concentrating. Therefore, they seem quiet and reserved. People often tell them they "think too much." Because they think deeply, they are talented and creative in music, art, writing and many other things. They usually are sensitive to others and are self-sacrificing. Often, they are persistent and perfectionists. As a result, they make friends cautiously and avoid being center-stage, but once they make friends they are very faithful. They set high standards for themselves and want things done exactly right. These students often are the artists, musicians and very smart people at school.

"Ed and Emily Easygoing." Ed and Emily are not outgoing, but they are not introverted either. They just have a steady attitude. They are laid back, easy-going and relaxed. Since they are agreeable, never in a hurry, and good listeners, they have many friends. They always look for the easy way of doing things, and avoid conflict at all costs, so rarely do people or circumstances upset them. Ed and Emily are always around watching what goes on, but they're rarely involved. Ed and Emily are watchers, not doers. They are listeners, not talkers.

POPULARITY

Popularity depends on belonging to the right group. But you can be popular with many different groups.

The Brains. This group exists on a different wave length than everybody else. Most people have trouble using a computer, but these people build them. You can recognize them by their raised eyebrows, four-syllable words, and books under both arms.

The Jocks. This group lives in the gym and out on the

playing field, working out and practicing. You can recognize them by their smell!

The Musicians. Musicians come in two groups, the band members and the chorus members — many are in both. These students are "talented." They're always whistling, humming and tapping to the rhythm of songs.

The Party-ers. These students live for the weekend. They hit every party possible on Friday and Saturday night. Somehow they manage to stay out of trouble. They are the ones who have the hardest time getting through Monday because of their weekend.

The Druggies. These students don't wait until the weekend. They get high on a daily basis. They can be recognized by their glassy eyes.

The Rowdies. They are the mischievous ones. They don't mean to cause problems. It's just that trouble follows them. You can recognize them in the middle of the cafeteria food fights.

The Straights. These are the average ordinary sort of students. They make up one of the largest groups of students. They can't be recognized because they're average, and they look like all the other straights.

The Uniques. This group contains all the students who are different. These students don't want to be like anyone else, and they try hard not to be. They often do wild and crazy things, even with their hair and clothes, just to stay different. They can be easily recognized because they are unlike everyone else.

THE PERFECT COMBINATION

Even if you already knew your perfect date, this section probably helped you think even more clearly about him or her. So, based on the Big Three, what is the combination for your perfect date?

Looks _____

_____

_____ .

Personality _____

_____
_____ .

Popularity _____

_____
_____ .

A REAL LOSER

Now that you have defined your perfect date, Bill wants you to meet his winner who turned out to be a loser. She was perfect: a California girl, five-and-a-half feet tall, medium build with blonde hair, fair complexion and blue eyes. She was the life of the party, but still a "straight." Bill's dream had come true, or so he thought. Listen to what he says about her:

"After getting up my nerve, I asked her out. She said 'yes' and everything went perfectly. We had a great time.

"I continued to ask her out, but after the first couple of dates I noticed something — she was selfish. She cared about herself much more than me, and it was obvious.

"But I continued to date her, because I thought I would be crazy to let go of someone who fit my picture of the perfect date. Besides, I might not find another perfect girl. So I hung on, hoping she would change.

"One night, after driving to her house, she started coming on to me physically. I didn't know what to do. The year before I had invited Jesus Christ into my heart, and one of the main ways He had been changing me was in my attitudes and conduct in dating relationships. I had committed myself to date according to God's plan, and I knew messing around would not honor Jesus Christ.

"All I could think was, *How can I get out of here?* I nervously looked at my watch and told my date that I had to get home. I walked her to the door and never asked her out again.

"*What went wrong?* I asked myself and God. *How could she be such a loser as a date? Will I ever find another per-*

fect girl, and if I do, how can I keep the same thing from happening again?"

WHAT THE BIG THREE MISS

Unfortunately, the Big Three (looks, personality and popularity) cover only the superficial qualities of people and completely miss the most important category of all — character. Character is everything a person is on the inside — especially his attitudes and maturity. It is often a result of the person's spiritual life and convictions. And that's what really counts!

Take Bill's dream date, for example. Outside, she had everything he thought was important, but inside, she was selfish and impure. All her positive outer qualities could not cover up those negative inner ones. As a result, their relationship did not last.

This is true in every relationship. On the outside, a person can be the best you have ever seen, but if he or she does not have positive character qualities, the relationship will be a real loser.

If you ignore the person's character, you'll bomb every time because the outside will not last. Beauty lies only at the surface of a person's body and fades with age, but character lives deep within a person and continues to get better and better with age. The qualities you appreciate in another person today will be even stronger and better twenty years from now, and even better forty years after that.

Many students think dating a person with all the outer qualities they desire is worth the price of putting up with negative character qualities. They continue to date, hoping for a change, and get drawn into a relationship. Because they're comfortable with the other person, they get married and put up with each other for two or three years.

One day, they look at their spouse and realize that the looks don't matter anymore. Neither does popularity. And even a great personality doesn't make up for the lack of character. Shocked, they finally admit that they really don't like this person. They see the person for what he or she is really like. With all the pretty wrapping aside, all that's left is the ugly inside.

This is not to say the outer qualities are not important. It's understandable that you want to date someone who looks his best. For example, a girl who braids her hair is all right — unless it is under her arms! A guy who brushes his teeth is fine — unless it is only once a month. Few people are attracted to someone who doesn't take care of himself. So, it is important to give proper attention to looking neat and smelling sweet.

But how can you see someone's character qualities?

WHO'S IN CONTROL?

Galatians 5:16-23 lists specific character qualities — both positive and negative.

> But I say, walk by the Spirit, and you will not carry out the desire of the flesh. For the flesh sets its desire against the Spirit, and the Spirit against the flesh; for these are in opposition to one another, so that you may not do the things that you please. But if you are led by the Spirit, you are not under the Law.
>
> Now the deeds of the flesh are evident, which are: immorality, impurity, sensuality, idolatry, sorcery, enmities, strife, jealousy, outbursts of anger, disputes, dissensions, factions, envyings, drunkenness, carousings, and things like these, of which I forewarn you just as I have forewarned you that those who practice such things shall not inherit the kingdom of God.
>
> But the fruit of the Spirit is love, joy, peace, patience, kindness, goodness, faithfulness, gentleness, self-control; against such things there is no law.

The Negatives

Verses 19-21 list the negative qualities, which are the works or the result of "the flesh." The flesh is that sinful part of everyone that says "Do your own thing." The attitude of the flesh is, "I'll do what I want to do, when I want to, with whom I want to, as long as I want to. And I'm not going to listen to anyone tell me otherwise!"

Before a person becomes a Christian, the flesh is constantly in control. This independent attitude continually exerts its influence. As a result, the person develops negative character qualities. Some people express these qualities more than others, but nevertheless they are there.

Look at each of the negative character qualities individually. After each quality is a definition and a question. Answer each question "yes" or "no" in light of a person you consider as a prospective date.

Immorality. Immorality means going "too far" physically. Remember the list in chapter 2? *Question:* Has your date recently been involved in immorality?

Impurity. Immorality deals with actions. Impurity deals with thoughts. Impurity means a person thinks about sex a lot. This shows up in what a person talks about, reads and watches on television. And thoughts are the basis of your actions. Impure thoughts lead to immoral actions. Pure thoughts lead to pure actions. *Question:* Does your date refer to sex a lot?

Sensuality. This trait bridges the gap between impurity and immorality. Sensuality means always thinking of how to satisfy sexual desires. *Question:* Does your date make plans so you can mess around physically?

Idolatry. Idolatry means loving something more than God. This can include people, popularity, power, prestige or possessions. *Question:* Does your date love anything more than Jesus Christ?

Sorcery. Sorcery means being involved in the occult — Satan-inspired activity. Common forms include magic, Ouija boards, horoscopes, tarot cards, automatic writing, fortune telling, drugs and séances. *Question:* Does your date experiment with the occult?

Enmities. Enmities mean to hate someone. Parents, teachers, and other students are often the object of this hate. *Question:* Does your date hate anyone?

Strife. Strife means the inability to get along with other people. *Question:* Is your date in conflict with others?

Jealousy. Jealousy means a bitter or resentful rivalry.

It causes your date to want to keep you away from others. Possessiveness and distrust are expressions of jealousy. *Question:* Does your date discourage you from having other friends?

Anger. Anger means hostility toward another person. The angry person gets upset if things don't go his way. *Question:* Does your date get upset easily?

Disputes. Disputes mean not giving in until a point is proven. People who dispute don't like to admit they are wrong. *Question:* Does your date have to have the last word all the time?

Dissensions. Dissensions are disagreements about opinions. They usually turn into arguments, and the emphasis is on who's right, not on keeping friendships. *Question:* Does your date argue a lot?

Factions. Factions are fights between two groups. *Question:* Does your date instigate fights with others?

Envying. Envying is wanting something that belongs to another. This could be possessions, abilities, positions, or anything else. *Question:* Does your date want things that belong to others?

Drunkenness. Drunkenness is drinking too much alcohol. The person drinks until alcohol controls his senses and abilities. *Question:* Does your date drink?

Carousing. Carousing means to "party." It means going to wild parties, drinking, and doing things you're ashamed of later. *Question:* Does your date "party?"

The Bible cautions you to avoid dating people who have these negative qualities. There are several reasons. First, these are all signs of self-centeredness, and God knows a self-centered person will not meet your needs. Remember, God is committed to giving you the best. Second, it might damage your reputation as a Christian. People would think things of you that aren't true. Third, it could hinder your relationship with Christ. You might be tempted to compromise. Because you want to please your date, you could give in and do something that would dishonor Christ and hurt your fellowship with God.

The Positives

After you become a Christian, you don't become instantly perfect. But when you receive Christ you do become a brand-new person on the inside (read 2 Corinthians 5:17). The Spirit of God enters you and begins to change you. One of the things He changes is your desires. With the old desires you please yourself, but with these new desires you please Jesus Christ.

Since the old desires still exist, you'll often struggle between which to obey. Your selfish desires and your godly desires pull you in different directions. Fortunately, God did not give you only the new desires. He also gave you a new power — the Spirit — to live according to those new desires. Therefore, when you choose to follow these new desires, new positive character qualities result.

Now read the following definitions from Galatians 5:22,23 and answer the questions as you did earlier.

Love. Love means commitment to another person, desiring the very best that God can give him. This commitment holds regardless of how it affects you. *Question:* Does your date consider others first?

Joy. Joy is an inner happiness. This happiness is not based on circumstances, but on a relationship with Jesus Christ. It results in an optimistic outlook, because Jesus really cares about you. *Question:* Does your date base his happiness on his circumstances?

Peace. Peace is the assurance that God has everything under control even when it doesn't look like it. To be relaxed under pressure provides freedom from fear and worry. *Question:* Is your date confident that God is in control?

Patience. Patience means the willingness to wait on the right timing. It means the person doesn't jump ahead of God, trying to make something happen. *Question:* Would your date wait to go out with you if your parents thought you should wait?

Kindness. Kindness means considering the needs of

others. It takes the time to reach out to others who are in need. It is an attitude of helping others. *Question:* Does your date reach out to others?

Goodness. Goodness means wanting to do what is right. The person sees the two choices and does what honors Christ. *Question:* Does your date seek to honor Jesus Christ?

Faithfulness. Faithfulness means dependability. The person follows through on his word, and always comes through even if it costs him. *Question:* Does your date fulfill his responsibilities?

Gentleness. Gentleness is being sensitive to another's emotional needs, seeking to listen and understand. *Question:* Does your date seek to understand you?

Self-control. Self-control means submitting your desires to God's desires. Self-control shows up in a person's eating and exercise. It is an ability to control all physical appetites, including sex. *Question:* Is your date in control of all his appetites?

God wants these qualities to be active not only in you, but also in the person you date. He knows only a person like this can truly make you happy. Before you even rate a person's looks, personality or popularity, you must determine what he is like on the inside.

Remember, these qualities are called "fruit." The older it gets, the more it matures. Therefore, you can't expect a person to be perfect in each of these areas. However, because of the possibility of spending the rest of your life with this person, you need to make sure that your date is controlled by the Spirit, not controlled by the flesh. Specifically, this means that he makes it a daily practice to confess his sins to God as well as to allow the Spirit to lead, fill and empower his life. This is vitally important in picking a winner.

ACTION SECTION

1. Think of someone you would like to date. Write his or her initials here. _____

2. Check these qualities you have seen in his or her life.

Works of the Flesh:

___ Immorality	___ Enmities	___ Dissensions
___ Impurity	___ Strife	___ Factions
___ Sensuality	___ Jealousy	___ Envyings
___ Idolatry	___ Anger	___ Drunkenness
___ Sorcery	___ Disputes	___ Carousings

Fruits of the Spirit:

___ Love	___ Patience	___ Faithfulness
___ Joy	___ Kindness	___ Gentleness
___ Peace	___ Goodness	___ Self-Control

3. Based on your evaluation, have you picked a winner?
   _____ Yes
   _____ No

4. If you are presently dating this person, how do you feel about your relationship after reading this chapter?
   _____ Right on target
   _____ Need to get to know him or her better
   _____ Need to break up

5. If you feel . . .
   Right on target, turn to chapter 4.
   The need to get to know him or her better, turn to chapter 4.
   Like you need to break up, turn to chapter 11.

6. Memorize Galatians 5:22,23.

4

Dating Non-Christians ♥

*L*IKE all girls, Susan wants to date. However, it seems like every weekend all she does is sit at home and watch TV with her parents and little brother. To make things worse, even her little brother goes out more than she does — and he's only eight. She used to go out more. But since she became a Christian a few months ago, she has been more selective about who she dates.

Then a friend calls to ask her to double date, but with a non-Christian. Susan knows him. She figures she'd better not go out with him. But it's been so long since she's had a date. As she thinks about it, her friend says that this guy is changing, that he doesn't hang around his old friends much anymore. Besides, says Susan's friend, maybe Susan can lead him to Christ.

Maybe her friend is right. Maybe she should go out as a witness to this guy. But she still doesn't feel right about it. Susan doesn't know what to do. She tells her friend that she will give her an answer before the weekend.

What should she do?

She prays about it that night. Then, the next day after school, Susan talks to Jan, an older Christian. Jan advises Susan from the Bible. She turns to 2 Corinthians 6:14-18:

> Do not be bound together with unbelievers; for what partnership have righteousness and lawlessness, or what fellowship has light with darkness? Or what harmony has Christ with Belial, or what has a believer in common with an unbeliever? Or what agreement has the temple of God with idols? For we are the temple of the living God; just as God said, "I will dwell in them and walk among them; and I will be their God, and they shall be my people. Therefore come out from their midst and be separate," says the LORD. "And do not touch what is unclean; and I will welcome you. And I will be a father to you, and you shall be sons and daughters to me," says the LORD Almighty.

Even though she really wants to go out, Susan decides not to.

Sometimes people's desires and God's desires come into conflict. It is hard to sacrifice what you want in order to please Christ. Everyone wants to make excuses, to show why his situation is an exception. Most of the excuses sound reasonable. Maybe you've heard, or even made, some of these excuses for dating a non-Christian:

He understands me.

She accepts me for who I am.

I haven't gone out in a long time, and I'm lonely.

There aren't any Christians I want to date.

Non-Christians have more fun than Christians.

Christian guys are wimps. They are too scared to ask anyone out.

She's nicer than the Christian girls I know.

He's really changing. He's not at all like he was.

I'm not going to marry her.

I'll go out with him only once or twice.

My friends want me to go and I'll disappoint them if I don't.

Everyone will think I'm stuck-up.

I don't know how to say "no" when a non-Christian asks me out.

I might lead him (or her) to Christ.

These excuses sound very logical, right? But remember, they're still excuses. They overlook the difference between Christians and non-Christians.

1 Corinthians 2:14 says, "The man without the Spirit does not accept the things that come from the Spirit of God, for they are foolishness to him, and he cannot understand them, because they are spiritually discerned" (NIV). This passage reveals that the excuse about the other person meeting your needs is not true because the non-Christian can't even understand the most important part of your life.

While you can have a good relationship with a non-Christian, even a good dating relationship, it can never be *the best* because non-Christians cannot understand the spiritual side of your life.

God wants you to be happy; He wants to protect you from harm. In Proverbs 6:27,28, He cautions, "Can a man take fire in his bosom and his clothes not be burned? Or can a man walk on hot coals and his feet not be scorched?" Dating non-Christians is like playing with fire. You can get burned.

Maybe God has limited your prospects to protect you from a bad relationship. Paul writes, "Do not be deceived, bad company corrupts good morals" (1 Corinthians 15:33).

The point of 2 Corinthians 6:14-18 is that Christians are to be different from non-Christians. One translation puts it this way: "Be ye not unequally yoked together with unbelievers" (King James). The phrase "yoked together" brings to mind two animals (not that you or your date are animals). Usually, two oxen, with a heavy wooden brace holding them together, plowed a field. "Unequally yoked" means that the animals are different, like an ox and a donkey.

In Deuteronomy 22:10 God says not to plow with an ox and a donkey together. He says this because He knows it doesn't work for obvious reasons: (1) the ox is stronger than the donkey, (2) the ox is faster than the donkey, and (3) the ox is less stubborn than the donkey. In the same way, God knows that a Christian and a non-Christian do not make good dating partners.

NOTHING IN COMMON

God didn't just say, "Don't date non-Christians." He gave specific reasons in 2 Corinthians 6:15.

Christians have *nothing in common* with non-Christians. That doesn't seem true. Don't you have the same classes, the same hobbies, the same friends, and play the same sports? Of course. But those are only what you *do,* not who you *are.* In God's eyes, who you are is most important. Now that you have Christ in your life, it's a whole different ball game.

The Living Bible translates 2 Corinthians 5:17, "When someone becomes a Christian he becomes a brand new person inside. He is not the same anymore. A new life has begun!"

Here are some ways you are different:

Lifestyles

Christians and non-Christians have different lifestyles. Verse 14 of 2 Corinthians asks, "What partnership have righteousness and lawlessness, or what fellowship has light with darkness?"

A Christian's tendency is to do what *Christ* wants him to do — that which is righteous and brings light into the world. The non-Christian's tendency is to do what *he* wants to do — that which is lawless and just adds darkness to the world.

For example, Dave was with his buddies recently at a friend's house. The parents were gone, so someone suggested they invite some girls over. The guys teased Dave, who is a Christian, by asking who he wanted to have over. But before he could even answer, one of the others said, "No way! You're a Christian!" How great that they knew he had a different lifestyle! He's committed to living in a way that pleases Jesus Christ, not his own desires.

This is another reason to choose carefully whom you will date. An immature Christian often can mislead others by following his own desire. This hurts more than a non-Christian doing the same, because you don't expect it from the Christian.

Loyalties

Christians have different loyalties. Verse 15 asks, "What harmony has Christ with Belial [the devil]?" Although he may not realize it, by not belonging to Jesus, a non-Christian's loyalty ultimately belongs to Satan. A Christian's loyalty belongs to Christ. Most non-Christians see themselves as doing their own thing, not hurting anyone; but Ephesians 2:2 says, ". . . you formerly walked according to the course of this world, according to the prince of the power of the air [the devil]. . ."

Loves

Christians have different loves. Verse 16 asks, "What agreement has the temple of God with idols?" Everyone loves something. What you love the most is what you worship. If you love anything or anyone more than Jesus Christ, you worship an idol.

Non-Christians worship many different idols — relationships, popularity, cars, sports and money. Some people worship themselves. Christians worship Jesus Christ only.

LEARNING THE HARD WAY

Listen to what one girl wrote about dating a non-Christian:

I thought he would fulfill needs I wanted met . . . I wanted — whether I would have admitted this or not — to be socially accepted. Being with him meant that I was seen with someone popular and maybe people would think I was like him . . . He filled an emotional need. He gave me attention and told me things I wanted to hear — I was special, pretty, lovable and important.

This was love to me. He made me feel good, therefore I thought I was in love. Unfortunately, my needs weren't met for very long . . . We grew farther and farther apart. Needless to say, I started feeling angry and frustrated.

What happened? It started off so good, but it ended in misery. This particular experience is like so many others. At first, dating a non-Christian may not seem any different. It takes time before the emptiness becomes apparent.

Generally, the relationship goes through three stages:

Stage 1: The Everything's-Great Stage. The relationship begins here. You meet a guy or a girl who sweeps you off your feet. You get chill bumps and heart throbs every time you're with him. You find out he's not a Christian, but you convince yourself this is an exception.

Stage 2: The We're-Just-Going-Through-A-Phase Stage. You've gotten to know each other well enough now so that his weaknesses are starting to show, but you're afraid of losing an exciting relationship, so you hold on to the hope that he will change.

Stage 3: The What-Went-Wrong? Stage. Your eyes are finally open. You feel miserable because you aren't as close to the Lord anymore. Confusion sets in because the relationship has gotten so messed up. You know you need to break up.

Many do break up. Some don't, though. As a result, they end up marrying non-Christians with the hope that they will change. When this happens, a ten-step breakdown often follows:

1. *Loneliness.* Because the non-Christian is dead spiritually, he cannot communicate with the spouse about the things that mean the most to the Christian.

2. *Disappointment.* The non-Christian said he would

change, but didn't.

3. *Mistrust.* Because of the lies and hurt, now it is hard to trust the non-Christian spouse.

4. *Pressure.* The Christian desperately wants the spouse to change so he begins to nag and preach.

5. *Resentment.* Because of the pressure to change, the spouse gets angry and goes further in the other direction.

6. *Separation/Divorce.* Since a non-Christian is looking out for his own needs, he leaves for someone or something "better."

7. *Guilt.* Feelings of guilt result from getting into this situation. The Christian feels like he's let everyone down — himself, his family and God.

8. *Depression.* All the joy is gone. All that's left are the scars and heartaches.

9. *Fear.* The Christian realizes that he will have to start life all over with nowhere to go. That frightens him. The future seems terribly bleak.

10. *The Next Generation.* Rarely do people think beyond themselves. Children suffer tremendously because of a wrong decision to marry.

Sound pretty negative? It is, but it doesn't have to be that way. You can get in on Christ-centered dating and experience the very best relationship imaginable!

Why, then, would a Christian date a non-Christian? Some Christians date non-Christians because:

- They enter the relationship before accepting Christ.
- They don't know any better — they haven't had the opportunity to learn what God's Word says about dating non-Christians.
- They mistakenly think their date is a Christian.
- They know better but keep rationalizing it until they convince themselves it's all right.
- They allow their feelings to get out of control and become emotionally involved.
- They are rebellious. They have deliberately chosen to

disobey what they know is right.

What if a non-Christian asks you out? First say "no, thank you," and then tell him about your commitment to Christ — in that order.

BREAKING UP

What if you're already dating a non-Christian? 2 Corinthians 6:17 says, "Therefore, come out from their midst and be separate." Regardless of how you got involved with dating a non-Christian, God wants you to separate. That means breaking up.

Breaking up is never easy. The emotional pain is terrible. But if you are committed to Jesus Christ as your Lord, you will pay any price to be obedient. Obedience is how you express your love for Jesus, and it is the way you will grow spiritually and emotionally.

So you're ready to obey, but how do you break up? Don't "dump on God" or anyone else. The choice is yours. Don't say you are breaking up because God, your youth minister or this book told you to do it. Assume responsibility for wanting to change the relationship. Don't take a "holier than thou" approach, either, saying, "Because I am committed to being a Christian I can no longer go out with a sinful creep like you."

Consider these helpful guidelines in breaking up with a non-Christian:

● Tell him or her that you want to grow in your personal relationship with Jesus Christ. If you have never talked about this before, this is an excellent opportunity to tell what you were like before you personally met Christ, how you accepted Christ as Savior and Lord, and what changes He has made and wants to make in you.

● Express to him or her the reasons your present dating relationship is not encouraging that growth. Be specific. For example, your date may want to get involved physically, or to watch suggestive movies and videos, or to have you spend time with him or her rather than attending church youth activities.

● This will probably be painful for you both, so be as gentle as possible but don't back down. Tears might flow because you will not be able to spend special time together like you did before. But in spite of the tears, follow through with your decision to break up.

● Accept the responsibility for any problems in the relationship that are your fault. If you were involved physically, ask forgiveness for your part of the problem.

If your date desires to commit his life to Christ because of your stand, do not counsel him. Instead direct him to your youth minister or a strong Christian. This will test his sincerity and keep you from continuing any emotional involvement.

If he makes a commitment to Christ, give him time to get established in this new relationship before dating again. This will give time to develop new priorities and habits. Also, it will enable you to see if the commitment is genuine.

THE RIGHT CHOICE

How can you make the right choice the first time or keep from having to break up with a non-Christian again? By making sure he is a real Christian *before* going out.

Never assume that someone is a Christian. Below are some questions to ask yourself to help determine whether someone is a follower of Christ. This is not judging a person, which is wrong, but it is trying to understand the person's spiritual condition. The way to tell the difference is in your attitude. The attitude of a person judging someone else is condemning. The attitude of a person trying to find out someone's spiritual health is patient, understanding, and sympathetic. This is discernment. The attitude behind discernment is always concerned love. Ask these questions about a potential date:

1. Does he claim to be a follower of Christ?
2. Do his actions and words back this up especially when you aren't around? Ask friends.
3. Does he have a desire to study the Bible, pray and

be with other Christians?

    4. Can he tell how Christ has changed him since accepting Christ?

    Answering questions like these will help you discern whether the person is a Christian. If you can honestly answer "yes" to all of these, you can be confident that dating this person would not bind you together with a non-Christian.

MEETING YOUR NEEDS

    When you choose to obey God's Word, He promises to meet your needs. 2 Corinthians 6:17,18 says, "I will welcome you. And I will be a father to you, and you shall be sons and daughters to Me." A father is committed to taking care of the needs of his children.

    A girl wrote, "It was very painful to part with him. I felt no one on this earth would ever love me like he did . . . (but) Christ gave me peace, comfort and love. Now my needs are truly met."

    This sums it up. If you trust God and obey His Word, He will meet all your needs in ways that only He can. Don't let fear keep you from experiencing God's best. Trust Him. He will not disappoint you.

    If you've reached this point in the book and you're not sure if you're a Christian, take time right now to read appendix A. It will help you either be sure you are, or learn how to become, a follower of Jesus Christ.

ACTION SECTION

1. Think of someone you would like to date. Write that person's initials here. _____

2. Is he or she a Christian?
    Yes   _____
    No   _____

Not sure ____

3. If yes, how do you know?

_____

_____

_____

4. Get to know this person well enough in friendly, public conversation to answer the four questions on page 57.
Answer to Question #1 _____
Answer to Question #2 _____
Answer to Question #3 _____
Answer to Question #4 _____

5. Memorize 2 Corinthians 6:14.

5

Getting Dates (Guys Only) ♥

SLOWLY, it builds, increasing day after day. First, it happens to one friend. Then another. And another. Finally, all your friends are dating. And you're still crouched in the blocks at the starting line. Frustration.

"When ya gonna get a date, shy guy?" they joke in the locker room. "Girls don't bite, ya know."

Well, relax. Once you've got the basics down (all discussed in the first four chapters), this chapter can help you get dates and end the frustration and embarrassment.

THE WRONG APPROACH

People have developed several approaches to getting dates since dating came into existence. Cavemen practiced the "knock 'em out" approach. They would spot an attractive girl, conk her over the head with a club, then drag her off on a date. But that's illegal now.

Another approach is "playing the odds." This method argues that if you ask enough girls out, sooner or later one will accept. You'd better have an alligator-skin ego, though, to be able to withstand repeated rejection, because you're going to get shot down a lot.

One student used this approach because he didn't understand girls very well. If one girl turned him down, he would immediately call another. Sometimes he called as many as a dozen or more girls before he got a date. He always wondered why they were turned off by his lack of sensitivity.

Another student advertised. He walked all over campus with a posterboard around his neck. The front had his phone number, and the back read, "Call if interested in going out." He didn't get any calls.

Another desperate guy sent a mass mailing to potential dates. He wrote a questionnaire and sent it to every girl in the school.

Name _____ Paste Recent Photo Here

Age _____

Phone Number _____

Interests _____
_____

Availability _____

On the back he stamped his name and address. The result — too much work for too little return.

The above approaches may sound worth a try, especially if you're desperate, but let's look at a better way.

PREPARING FOR SUCCESS

Most good things don't just happen. A lot of time and effort go into preparing for success. Guys, the same is true of dating. From Proverbs 3:5,6 you find two things that prepare you for successful dating. What are they?

> Trust in the Lord with all your heart, and do not lean on your own
> understanding. In all your ways acknowledge Him, and He will make
> your paths straight.

1. Trust Jesus Christ With Your Dating

What a powerful challenge these verses offer because
dating causes one of a guy's biggest worries. If you're like
most guys, your mind is constantly filled with questions like:

What does she think of me?

Will she go out with me?

What if she says she doesn't want to go out with me?

How will I get a car?

Do I have enough money to take her out?

Will I ever find the right girl?

Ever find yourself asking these questions? If you have
red blood and it's still moving through your body, you have.
They consume a lot of mental energy, right? Makes you real
uptight, too. But it's not just dating that does this.

Whenever people try to depend on their own strength
and understanding apart from God, they worry. Why do you
think there are so many headache and indigestion commercials
on television?

God saved you to give you a new and different life,
and part of that life is being relaxed about dating. He wants
dating to be fun, not a pain. This is possible only when you
trust Jesus Christ with your dating relationships. That means
you give Jesus the responsibility for your dating. Put Him in
charge of getting you ready to date and helping you find the
right girl. If somebody is going to worry about your dating,
let it be God.

Genesis 24 has a great example of this kind of trust.
Take a few minutes to read over that now. A single guy named
Isaac sat in a field, meditating. He wasn't frantically trying to
find his future wife, because he had turned that responsibility
over to God. He probably prayed for God to show him that special girl, but he wasn't worried about it. He had placed his

trust in God to bring her across his path, and he was confident God would come through. He did! Did he just sit back and passively cool it? No. Isaac made himself available, talking to the Lord, praying for guidance, and acting on what God showed him.

Isaac's approach illustrates the important role God must play in dating. Over and over, students experience frustration about their dating or lack of it. They worry because they try to run their dating lives by themselves. After they turn their dating over to the Lord, they become confident and calm, because God has taken control.

2. Obey Jesus Christ in Your Dating

To "acknowledge Him in all your ways" means to obey Jesus in everything you do and say. In other words, you decide to follow Him where He leads. This sometimes causes conflict, because what you want and what Christ wants may be different. This was painfully true for one student.

Tom had dated the same girl for four years, despite wrestling with surrendering his dating relationship to God. He knew that God would change what he did on dates, so he resisted.

One night, at 2 A.M., Tom finally decided to give Jesus Christ complete control of his dating.

The next day, though, his girlfriend wasn't too excited when he told her. In fact, she got angry. Because of her response, Tom had to break up with her.

He knew what he did was right, but it tore him up. He couldn't understand why God would let him suffer. But God had something better. Tom's job: obey.

When you trust and obey Jesus Christ, "He will make your paths straight." He will show you who to date and how to date to make sure you get in on His very best.

That is exactly what happened to Tom. Later, he wrote:

You know, the Lord did it. He gave me something better. I thought I needed another girlfriend, so I waited and prayed and prayed. But God gave me what I really needed — a better life.

The Lord has blessed me more than I could have imagined. Before my decision to surrender my dating to Him, I'd been having a hard time obeying His will. After that choice, though, it got so easy. Now, I can't imagine disobeying like I did before. All because I gave Him everything in my life and was obedient to Him.

I gave Him what I thought was the best and in return He gave me what He knew was the best.

GO FOR THE BEST

Do you want to experience God's best for your dating? Let's look at some ways that can happen.

Confess. Ask God to forgive you for not trusting Him. Tell Him that you are sorry for not believing He wants the best for you and for trying to run this area of your life.

Commit. Write out on a piece of paper a commitment expressing your desire for God to control your dating from now on. Sign it, date it and look at it frequently. This example can help:

> *Lord Jesus, in the past I have depended on my own understanding and run my dating life the way I thought was best. Today I am turning this area of my life over to you. With all my heart, I am committing myself to trust you to lead me and guide me. In Jesus' name, Amen.*
>
> Name _____
> Date _____

Pray. After you have committed yourself to let Christ control your dating, then don't worry about it again. Worry is the opposite of trust. Philippians 4:6,7 says:

> Be anxious for nothing, but in everything by prayer and supplication with thanksgiving let your requests be made known to God. And the peace of God, which surpasses all comprehension, shall guard your hearts and your minds in Christ Jesus.

If you catch yourself worrying, stop immediately and write down what is bothering you. Then pray and talk to God about the problem until you have a peace that He will take care of you.

Obey. Determine to obey God every day. When what you want differs from what God wants, follow His instructions. Don't give in to your selfish desires even in the smallest way, regardless of the pain.

As you trust and obey Jesus Christ, He will make your paths straight and you will experience the very best in dating — better than you can imagine.

U.P.S. STRATEGY

"It's great to know this stuff," you say, "but I need to know how to get a date. What can I do to get a girl to go out with me?"

All right, we promised guidelines for getting dates. So now, get your pen and paper ready. Poise yourself on the edge of your seat. You are about to be exposed to the U.P.S. Strategy, so called because it always delivers! It consists of ten steps.

Step 1: Look Up

Identify the girls you're interested in dating. If you don't know who you are after, you'll never catch her.

There are several ways to do this. One student looked through all the registration cards after a church party. The staff had asked everyone to fill out their name, address and phone number so the church could contact everyone for future activities. That's exactly what this guy had in mind — future activities. He picked out the names of the four girls most attractive to him. It took him a couple of months to get up the nerve, but now he's dating the girl he considered the best of the bunch.

Another option: Write down the names of girls you know and whom you think would be fun to date. Once you have made a list, pick out the girl you want to date the most. Then gather as much information about her as possible without being obvious. Find out:

Is she a committed Christian?

What's her character like?

Who are her closest friends?

What classes is she taking?

What activities is she involved in at school?

What are her hobbies?

Finding out what she's like before you go out with her can protect you from some bad experiences. For example, on weekends she may be a lady wrestler who eats raw meat. If you find this out beforehand, you save yourself from some serious mat burns.

Knowing a few things about her can help when you call her, too. You will have several topics to talk about and will know how to guide the conversation.

Step 2: Psyche Up

Once you have done your homework, call her. Sounds easy. Let's face it, you're probably nervous, real nervous. Even the guys who appear totally cool on the outside panic on the inside. Everyone is afraid of making a mistake like, "Hello, Barbara? This is movies. How would you like to go to the John with me?"

Before you call, pray. Ask Jesus to keep your voice from shaking and help you have a great conversation. Then go for it!

Step 3: Call Up

Call at least three days in advance. Why? To show her consideration and thoughtfulness. Many guys call girls at the last minute and offend them. So show her you're different — a gentleman. It will make her feel important. She will know that you planned ahead. And she will realize that you chose her first. The rule is, the bigger the date (what you are going to do, not her weight), the sooner you call.

If you call, use proper phone etiquette. Instead of yelling, "Hey, put Mary on the phone!" say, "Hello, this is John. May I speak to Mary, please?" If her parents answer the phone, this touch of class will set you apart in their minds. If she answers, she will feel respected.

Step 4: Open Up

During the first part of the conversation tell a few things about yourself to break the ice. But don't brag. Talk about a big turn-off — bragging is it.

Make a list of a few subjects to talk about to avoid long pauses in the conversation. For example:

- activities at school
- the latest ball game
- recent happenings at school
- the band concert
- school elections
- the new yearbook
- activities at church

Laughter has a great way of breaking the ice and making people feel comfortable. Use humor when appropriate. If you use humor, make sure it is funny to someone else besides yourself. It's not a joke if nobody laughs, and few things are worse than a bad joke.

Step 5: Listen Up

You do not want to do all of the talking. Ask her about herself. A list of prepared questions is helpful. You may want to include questions like:

Classes
- What classes are you taking?
- Which do you like the best?
- Which is the most fun? Why?
- Who would I know in some of your classes?

Activities
- What activities are you involved in?
- What are some of the things you do in these activities?

- Do you hold any offices?
- How long have you belonged?
- What do you enjoy about them?

Hobbies

- What are some of your hobbies?
- How did you get started?
- Is it hard to learn?
- What are some of the things you have done?

Family

- What is your family like?
- Do you have any brothers and sisters? Ages?
- Are you close to them?
- Does your family do a lot together?

Church

- Where do you go to church?
- What things has your youth group done?
- Why did you start going to church?

Christ

- When did you become a Christian?
- How did it happen?
- How do you feel about your commitment now?

You don't want to grill her like a lawyer, so have an idea of what you would like to know about her, and ask a few relevant questions. These questions should help you think of some good ones to ask.

Step 6: Set Up

After talking for a while both of you should feel comfortable. Now, pop the question.

No! Not "Will you marry me?" but "Will you go out with me?"

In asking, never have the attitude: "You wouldn't want to go out with me, would you?" If you ask like that she will think you have a disease.

Nor should you have the attitude: "Of course you would like the privilege of going out with me since I am God's gift to women. When would you like to pick me up?"

One of the best ways to pop the question is to ask it like this: "You know, Hermanatica, I've enjoyed talking with you. Would you like to get together Tuesday of next week at 3 P.M. to look for lost golf balls at Frank's Miniature Golf? That way we could get to know each other better."

When you ask her, always include *when* and *what* you plan to do specifically. Never just ask if she would like to go out. If she thinks you are a turkey, you have left her only two options: (1) She can go out and be miserable, or (2) she can turn you down and hurt your feelings.

Giving her the time of the date gives her a polite way of excusing herself if she doesn't want to go. If she says she is committed, it's OK to say, "Maybe we could go another time," and see what she says. But don't fish for another date. If she wants to go out with you, she will apologize and let you know she would like for you to ask her out again. She might even offer nights when she is available. If this happens, don't waste any time in getting the date. Nail it down on the spot.

Planning the date ahead of time shows the girl you have thought this date through. This makes her feel special. Plan the date so that there are plenty of opportunities to talk. For example, going to the movies on a first date is one of the worst places for getting to know each other. But playing Frisbee in the park offers plenty of time to talk.

Consider setting up a group date for the first date. It relaxes the pressure and often girls are more willing to go out in that situation. (See chapter 7, "Dating Creatively.")

Step 7: Hang Up

No, not before you get an answer. And if she says "yes," don't answer "Really?" Say, "Great!" Then set up a time to call again to confirm the plans. She may need to ask her parents' permission.

After these things are nailed down, tell her you enjoyed talking and look forward to seeing her. *Then* put the receiver on the hook.

Step 8: Fire Up

Go ahead. Let out that yell of victory. But first make sure you've completed Step 7 — hang up the phone!

Step 9: Fix Up

This step involves fixing up your car and your body. Both could probably use a good cleaning. As for the car, be sure to clean out all of your junk, including your guitar case, school books, broken stereo speaker, football, tennis shoes, the food from last month's camping trip, and all the sacks filled with drinking cups, french fry bags and hamburger boxes. And don't forget your gym clothes from last quarter!

After the car is emptied of all the big stuff, wash, wax, vacuum, and spray it with disinfectant. It would be terrible if your date died after being attacked by some strange fungus in your car, so clean it well.

Your body will need as much attention as your car. Strategic areas include: Your hair — be sure to get all the grease out. Your ears — get the wax out. Your nose — make sure the hairs don't hang below your nostrils. Your teeth — give 'em a good brushing and flossing. Your complexion — get as many of the white ones and black ones as you can without looking like a track team ran over your face. Your hands — clean the dirt out from under your nails. Your pits — scrub hard and use lots of deodorant (not too much, though, or you'll make her pass out). If you plan to sweat a lot, use it three times, but no more.

If you clean all these well, you will be in good shape. On your way out take one last look in the mirror to make sure everything is OK.

Step 10: Pick Up

At last! You are ready to take her out. Only you need to meet her parents. Don't worry! Just be on time, go to the door and be yourself (or rather, your best self). You need to talk with them for several minutes the first time you meet them. If you don't want to talk much, ask the parents questions. As long as they talk, you don't have to. Here are some questions you might ask:

- What kind of work do you do?
- How long have you lived in the area?
- What brought you to this area?
- Stand up and compliment her without going overboard.
- Ask her folks what time she needs to be home.
- Tell them you enjoyed meeting them (even if you didn't).
- Go out and have a great time.

ACTION SECTION

1. Write out one worry you have about dating, then write out beside it how Jesus can take care of this if you will let Him.

_____

_____

_____

2. If you have not allowed Jesus to have first place in your dating, confess that to Him and write out a prayer dedicating this area of your life to His Lordship.

_____

_____

_____

3. Name the girls you want to go out with. Write down what you know about them.

(A) _____

_____

(B) _____

_____

(C) _____

_____

4. Check which way you will get psyched up:

_____ Stand in front of the mirror and repeat twenty times, "I CAN DO IT!!!"

_____ Have your best friend tell you how much women love you.

_____ Remember all the times girls have said "yes" to going out with you.

_____ Ask God to give you confidence.

5. Write down exactly what you will say when someone on the other end of the phone says "hello."

_____

_____

6. What three interesting things can you talk about to get the conversation going?

_____

_____

_____

7. What are three good questions to ask the girl about herself?

_____

_____

_____

8. Write down the "what" and "when" of the date you want to take her on.

_____

_____

9. What are you going to say to end the conversation when she says "yes"?

_____

_____

How will you respond if she says "no"? (Don't be cruel — or a wimp!)

_____

_____

10. Write down how long it will take you to wash your car and your body. _____ What time will you need to start in order to be ready on time? _____

11. What questions can you ask her parents when you pick your date up?

_____

_____

12. Memorize Proverbs 3:5,6.

6

Getting Dates (Girls Only) ♥

A NOTHER Saturday night, and after watching one more rerun of a rerun, you feel stranded on Gilligan's Island, spaced out by Star Trek, and swamped by The Love Boat.

"Saturday nights are for dates," you scream, "not for reruns!"

Everyone else is out with that special guy, it seems. And you? Oh, sometimes you go to a football or basketball game with your friends. But mostly you sit home with your parents and little brother watching TV.

Boredom soon becomes depression. You sulk to your room, close the door, listen to sad music, and use a year's supply of tissues.

Around 9:30 P.M., you call an understanding friend and have a pity party, complaining about the sad state of affairs. By the time you hang up it's time to go to bed, which now is buried under the used tissues. You go to bed hoping that next week might be different. Maybe *someone* will ask you out.

Sound familiar? Actually, the sad person above doesn't have to be you. How do you go about getting a guy's attention? Read on!

As always, the Bible has the answer. The apostle Peter assured women in 1 Peter 3:3,4 that they could be attractive in more ways than one:

> And let not your adornment be external only — braiding the hair, and wearing gold jewelry, and putting on dresses; but let it be the hidden person of the heart, with the imperishable quality of a gentle and quiet spirit, which is precious in the sight of God.

These verses reveal four ways to get the right guy to date you for the right reasons.

LOOK YOUR BEST

In verse 3, notice the word "only." This means you shouldn't ignore your appearance. It says, concentrate on your inner beauty as well as your outer appearance.

Looking your best physically is important, because God created your physical body and He said that it was good. To not take care of yourself is like never cleaning your room. Pretty soon it looks like a pig pen.

Taking care of yourself is also important because other people are grossed out when you don't take care of yourself. Imagine a guy being attracted to a girl who never brushed her hair, blew her nose, brushed her teeth, washed her arm pits or shaved her legs.

Looking your best is important, but difficult. Why? Because friends put pressure on you to overdo the physical. The conversation in front of the mirror in the restroom makes you feel out of it if you don't dress and talk like the others. The "jock table" in the cafeteria rating the girls who pass by doesn't help either.

Because of the pressure to conform, many girls begin to wear clothes that are suggestive — shirts too loose or pants too tight, tops cut too low or skirts too high, "short" shorts, halter tops, see-through blouses and next-to-nothing bathing suits.

When asked about this, girls say, "It's the latest style," or "Everybody else is wearing them," or "It's summer."

But to overdo it gives guys the wrong impression. They think you are on the inside what you look like on the outside. Clothes that draw unnecessary attention to your figure communicate *physical signals.* Like a billboard advertising a product, everybody looks at you. These impressions last.

The way you dress is important, because the way you attract a guy is the way you keep him. If his attraction to you is based on your looks, he will constantly compare you to other girls. Since looks don't last, he won't either. The moment a better-looking girl comes along, he'll be gone.

Another reason not to overdo the way you dress is that the slightest suggestion of a girl's physical features can cause some guys' imaginations to run wild. Many girls say that's the guy's problem. Much of it is, but listen to the way one woman expressed it:

> I can remember thinking, *Well, it's not my fault if they can't keep their eyes off of me and on the Lord. They just aren't spiritual enough. Why should I have to change just because they are weak?*
> But the Lord showed me that it *was* my fault. I was responsible for causing my brother to stumble and it had to change. Once I saw the damage my selfishness was doing to others and to the Lord, I was really ashamed of myself and embarrassed that I had been representing Jesus in such an unbecoming way.[1]

That's the negative side of communicating through your physical appearance. But what are the positive ways?

REFLECT CHRIST IN YOUR APPEARANCE

Paul wrote, "Likewise, I want women to adorn themselves with proper clothing, modestly and discreetly, not with braided hair and gold or pearls or costly garments; but rather by means of good works, as befits women making a claim to godliness" (1 Timothy 2:9,10).

Clothes that honor Jesus Christ look "modest and discreet." That is, they don't draw unnecessary attention to any particular part of your body.

Don't get the wrong idea and go to an extreme, though. The Bible is not advocating wearing burlap bags and no make-up. It is, however, pointing to a balance. Pretty clothes and make-up are not wrong. But girls who are committed to Jesus Christ will reflect Him in the way they wear their clothes and make-up.

Ask yourself these questions to determine how much emphasis you place on your physical appearance:

- Are you considered a trend-setter — usually the first to buy the latest style?
- Do you spend a lot of time and money shopping for or looking at new clothes?
- Are you always thinking about what you're going to wear?
- Do you enjoy turning heads?[2]
- Do you spend longer than one hour getting ready to go out?
- Do you get upset if you are not as nicely dressed as someone else?
- Do you look at yourself every time you pass a mirror?

If you answered "yes" to any of these questions, then it's possible that you put too much emphasis on your external appearance.

How, then, can you look your best physically without overdoing it?

Commit yourself to dress in a way that honors Christ. Go through your wardrobe with a mature Christian woman and decide which outfits are most appropriate and look best on you. Discard the clothes that are too tight, too low-cut, too transparent or expose too much. Buy clothing in the future that you know honors Jesus Christ. Choose clothes that enhance the natural beauty God has given you but are not suggestive.

Learn to put on your make-up in a way that compliments your skin tone, and the color of your hair and eyes. Determine what colors brighten your face.

Change the physical features that you consider unattractive, if possible. For example, if you are overweight, go on a diet. Stay away from junk food. It bulges your figure and mars your complexion. Eliminating salt and sugar will do wonders for your weight, too. Remember: Eat it today, wear it tomorrow! A moment on the lips, forever on the hips. Get plenty of rest and exercise to keep your body in shape.

Accept yourself the way God has made you if you have unchangeable features (like large ears or unshapely feet) that you consider ugly. Stare at a photo of the world's highest-paid model. Look over her face and body inch by inch. Perfect, right? No zits. No cellulite. Ask her, though, and she'll tell you — faster than you can listen — ten things she'd change about her looks. No one ever has a perfect body, so change what you can and ask God to help you accept what you can't change.

Focus on positive thoughts about yourself. Your face and body will reflect how you feel about yourself.

INNER BEAUTY

1 Peter 3:4 continues, "But let it be the hidden person of the heart, with the imperishable quality of a gentle and quiet spirit, which is precious in the sight of God."

Looking your best physically is important, but Peter emphasizes that what is "precious in the sight of the Lord" is inner beauty.

In 1 Samuel 16:7 God says, "Do not look at his appearance or at the height of his stature . . . for God sees not as man sees, for man looks at the outward appearance, but the Lord looks at the heart."

Inner beauty is a priority to God. He wants you to reflect His Son, Jesus Christ, through you — from the inside out. Concentrate on your inner beauty.

Inner beauty is a priority to a godly guy. He is looking for a winner and will carefully consider your character — what you are like on the inside. You cannot expect to date a winner unless you're a winner, too.

Inner beauty is more important than your outer beauty. Your ugly big toe will always be ugly, but your ugly spirit and habits can change through Christ.

What steps can you take to develop your inner beauty? These hints will get you started. And as you keep going you will reflect Jesus more and more.

(Okay, guys, we know you're also reading this chapter to get the scoop on girls. So pay attention to this section; it's important for you, too! Just substitute the word "character" for "beauty" and take these tips to heart. The most important priority to a godly woman is a man's Christ-like inner character).

Learn to Pray

Prayer creates beauty because it puts you in communication with God. As you learn the following facets of prayer, His beauty will blossom in you.

● *Praise.* "I will bless the Lord at all times; His praise shall continually be in my mouth" (Psalm 34:1). To praise God means you tell Him how great He is. Read the Bible and write down specific attributes of God, then praise Him for His love, power, holiness and other characteristics.

● *Appreciation.* "Through Him then, let us continually offer up a sacrifice of praise to God, that is, the fruit of lips that give thanks to His name" (Hebrews 13:15). Appreciation is giving thanks for something you received. Express your appreciation to God for the wonderful things He has given you.

● *Confession.* "If we confess our sins, He is faithful

and righteous to forgive us our sins and to cleanse us from all unrighteousness" (1 John 1:9). Confession means to agree with God, whether it is positive or negative. Each day confess positive things the Bible says about you. For example, remind yourself each morning that you are God's person (Galatians 3:26,27). Also, confess to God immediately whenever you commit a sin. Agree with God that it was wrong. Tell Him you are sorry.

• *Petition.* "Until now you have asked for nothing in my name; ask and you shall receive that your joy may be made full" (John 16:24). This means to pray for yourself. Ask God to change those things in your life that need to be changed. Ask Him to work in and through your life.

• *Intercession.* "Far be it from me that I should sin against the Lord by ceasing to pray for you" (1 Samuel 12:23). Petition is prayer for yourself and intercession is prayer for others. Pray for at least one family member and two friends each day.

Get Into God's Word

Knowing God's Word creates beauty because you begin to make God's thoughts your thoughts. There are five ways to do this.

• *Listen to God's Word.* "Blessed is he who reads and those who hear the words of the prophecy, and heed the things which are written in it; for the time is near" (Revelation 1:3). Hearing God's Word taught each week helps you to grow as a person. Make it a priority to be at Sunday school and church every week. Taking notes helps you to pay attention better and remember more.

• *Read God's Word.* Make a goal to read part of the Bible every day (Revelation 1:3). Read before you go to school or before you go to bed. You can start with the Gospel of John.

• *Study God's Word.* "Be diligent to present yourself approved to God as a workman who does not need to be ashamed, handling accurately the word of truth" (2 Timothy

2:15). When you read God's Word you gain an overall perspective on what it says. Studying it helps you dig in and discover specifics. The best way to do this is by setting aside one time each week to study your Sunday school lesson. When you do this, you will get a lot more out of the class as well.

● *Memorize God's Word.* "Thy word I have treasured in my heart, that I may not sin against Thee" (Psalm 119:11). Each week find one verse from your reading or studying that means a lot to you. Write it on an index card. Carry it around with you. Memorize it word for word during the week.

● *Meditate on God's Word.* "But his delight is in the law of the Lord, and in His law he meditates day and night. And he will be like a tree firmly planted by streams of water, which yields its fruit in its season, and its leaf does not wither; and in whatever he does, he prospers" (Psalm 1:2,3). As you hear, read, study and memorize God's Word, think about what it is saying. Take five minutes each day for focused thought on how it applies to you. Put what you learn into practice that day.

Obey Jesus Christ

"He who has my commandments, and keeps them, he it is who loves Me; and he who loves me shall be loved by My Father, and I will love him, and will disclose Myself to him" (John 14:21). Whenever you learn something God wants you to do, do it. Obedience is allowing Jesus Christ to be Lord of your life.

Spend Time With Other Christians

"And let us consider how to stimulate one another to love and good deeds, not forsaking our own assembling together, as is the habit of some, but encouraging one another; and all the more, as you see the day drawing near" (Hebrews 10:24,25). It is hard to grow spiritually by yourself. You need others. Find Christian friends who understand you and can encourage you. If possible, find an older, more mature Christian woman. Ask her to show you how you can grow in your spiritual maturity.

Share Christ With Others

"For God has not given us a spirit of timidity, but of power and love and discipline. Therefore do not be ashamed of the testimony of our Lord" (2 Timothy 1:7,8). You experience inner growth every time you tell others about your relationship with Christ. Telling others about Christ is called witnessing. This telling involves two parts — what you say and how you live. You must have both to be effective.

As you follow these steps, you will find yourself becoming more and more like Jesus. Your inner beauty will develop to its fullest.

A FRIEND AND NOT A FLIRT

1 Peter 3:4 goes on to say, "But let it be the hidden person of the heart, with the imperishable quality of a gentle and quiet spirit, which is precious in the sight of God."

This verse emphasizes a gentle and quiet spirit. A person with a gentle spirit is someone kind and considerate toward others (i.e., someone who is a friend). A person with a quiet spirit is someone who trusts God to bring things to pass (i.e., is not a flirt).

A girl can get a guy's attention — and a date — in two ways: (1) You can be a flirt, a girl who makes insincere advances by using sexual attraction to get a guy's attention.[3] Or, (2) you can be a friend. Remember, Christ-centered dating builds a growing relationship between a guy and a girl which honors Jesus Christ by putting the other's needs first.

Because you must wait for a guy to ask you out, sometimes you have to wait longer than you want. Wanting to speed things up, you might slip into trying to make things happen. Flirting is the natural way to get his attention and make things happen.

Don't misunderstand. An outgoing personality is not flirting. Flirting communicates more than friendliness. It gives a guy the wrong impression by focusing the relationship on the physical.

Some girls flirt by calling guys on the phone, "just to talk." This flatters a guy, but it usually causes him to lose respect for her. Guys appreciate challenges. A girl who calls a guy comes across as an "easy win." For a while he enjoys it, but the chances of a long-term relationship are slim.

Some girls go as far as to ask a guy for a date. Although she may get the date she wants, her method carries with it some consequences. A girl who takes responsibility for starting a relationship one day can easily find herself going steady with a guy who abandons his role as the leader of the relationship. He reaches a point where he allows his girlfriend to handle everything. Soon, she can begin to resent her do-nothing boyfriend.

As always, you have an alternative — develop a friendship. When your friendship attracts a guy, you start your dating relationship on a solid foundation. Then it can build. But when you start it with flirting, its foundation is weak. As you try to build it, it crumbles.

A fine line exists between flirting and friendship. It takes discretion to recognize the difference. Discretion is the ability to know whether you act from friendship or flirting. Proverbs 11:22 talks about women who lack this: "As a ring of gold in a swine's snout, so is a beautiful woman who lacks discretion."

The proper approach to get a guy's attention is to be his friend, not a flirt. Ladies, which foundation are you building on?

If you have read this far, we're sure you want to learn to be a friend, not a flirt. Let's look at some practical friendship factors. And guys, make sure you pay attention to this part also! You, too, can apply this in your relationship with girls.

Factor 1: Get to Know Him

Ask yourself these questions and write the answers in a notebook.

- What are his likes and dislikes?
- Who are his friends?
- What are his activities?
- What is his family like?
- Where does he go to church?
- What is his relationship like with the Lord?

Factor 2: Listen to Him

When he talks, listen to what he says. Don't think about what you will say next. Remember what he tells you. Concentrate on listening to him.

Factor 3: Understand Him

Obviously, guys respond differently from girls in how they think and feel. Try to picture yourself in his situation when he is talking. Look for what he says underneath the words. Try hard to understand the feelings behind his words. Repeat back to him what he has told you to see if you have really understood him. Study him so you know what he is *really* like.

Factor 4: Focus Your Attention on Him

When he talks, look at his eyes. Don't glance here and there. Don't get distracted by other people or noises or music. But watch out: Those beautiful eyes of yours can communicate too much too soon. Keep the relationship a friendship!

Factor 5: Express Admiration

Tell him when you see qualities in his life that you admire. Don't flatter him, but express the specific godly qualities that you see in his life. Tell him why you admire the qualities. For example, "I admire your determination. You never give up on your goals. I admire that because a determined man can accomplish great things in his life." Point out his inner qualities, rather than his physical appearance.

Factor 6: Encourage Him

Point out his strengths and successes. When he fails, let him know you still believe in him. Comfort him when he is down and discouraged.

Factor 7: Serve Him

Look for ways to meet his needs. Do little things for him. Birthdays make good excuses to do something special for him. Again, be careful of overdoing.

Factor 8: Pray for Him

Each day, pray for him. Pray for more than a date with him. Ask him to mention specific things you can pray for. Pray scriptural prayers for him like Ephesians 1:15-19, 3:14-20, Philippians 1:9-11, and Colossians 1:9-12.

Factor 9: Give Him Room

Give your expectations of dating him to the Lord. It may take months before he asks you out, *if he ever does.* Concentrate on your friendship and wait.

Factor 10: Avoid Jealousy

One day he may tell you he has a date with your best friend. Don't blow it! Keep your emotions under control. You are his friend first. Hang in there.

You can only build a lasting relationship with a guy who goes out with you for who you are, and not with one who takes you out for what you will do. The friendship route moves a lot slower than the flirting route, but it gets you to your ultimate destination — a healthy, caring relationship.

BEFORE YOU SAY "YES"

Your dependence on God while the relationship develops is very important. 1 Peter 3:4 points to that dependence on God: "But let it be the hidden person of the heart, with the imperishable quality of a gentle and quiet spirit, which is precious in the sight of God."

Girls, you may have to wait a long time before a guy asks you out. Guys pick up signals slowly. If they didn't, they would ask girls out more often.

But one day the guy you have always wanted to date will finally ask you out. This is when the dependence on God that you've been cultivating in your life will show. What do you say? The obvious answer is "Yes!" Right?

No! Not necessarily. Don't assume that you should automatically say "yes" if a handsome, popular, mannerly man of God asks you out. Does the Lord want you to go out with him now? Is this the right time to go out? You need to bring this before God. Pray. You don't have to pray for a week before giving the guy an answer. But pray about it seriously. Tell him you will let him know the next day.

The same holds true even if a creep asks you out. Pray about it. If a guy follows Christ and passes the test in chapter 3, then you should still pray about it. God may want you to go out with him to minister to him, or to teach you something through him.

HOW TO SAY "NO"

If you don't believe you are to go out with a guy, say "no" as soon as you have prayed about it. The longer you put it off, the harder it becomes to repond to him. If you have trouble saying "no," ask your parents for help. Tell them you are having a hard time saying "no" and ask them if you can use them to protect you. Then, tell the guy that you and your parents decided it was best not to go out.

Don't feel guilty about saying "no" if you don't want to go out with a guy. Just express your appreciation to him for asking you and say, "No, thank you, I would rather not go out with you." He may react negatively — you have wounded his ego. Forgive him if he does not act like a gentleman when turned down. But feel free to decline his invitation. Because, after all, that's what it is: an invitation.

Don't become frustrated if you don't see instant success from living by these principles. Don't allow impatience to rip you off. Be willing to wait on God, who has already committed Himself to your very best.

ACTION SECTION

1. Answer the questions on page 78. Any "yes" answers? What steps will you take to deal with these?

    a. _____

    b. _____

2. What steps do you need to take to look your best in your outer appearance?

_____

_____

3. What steps do you need to take to improve your inner beauty?

_____

_____

_____

4. Write out in your own words the difference between a flirt and a friend. _____

_____

_____

5. Write down the initials of a guy you want to go out with. _____ What steps can you take to be a better friend to him? _____

_____

_____

6. Write down the words you will use to turn down someone you don't want to date. _____

_____

_____

7. How long are you willing to wait to go out with the right guy — the one God wants you to date? _____

8. Memorize 1 Peter 3:3,4.

7

Dating Creatively (Guys Only) ♥

*D*INNER, then a movie? Or a movie, then dinner? No wonder girls are always dieting. That's all guys can ever seem to think of for a date.

Dating is in a rut for a lot of reasons. First, guys tend to think about their own needs too much — dinner (my stomach) and movie (relax and don't have to talk). They enjoy it and figure their date enjoys it, too. But a girl's interests revolve around more than just her stomach.

Second, guys think they have to spend a lot of money on a girl for her to have a good time. Wrong again, guys! Most girls date you not for what you do for them, but for who you are. They think guys are the greatest!

You don't believe it? There's proof. Ask any girl what the number one topic of conversation is when girls get together. If she is honest, she will say, "Guys!" They talk about guys, dream about guys, and would do almost anything to go out with guys — without you having to spend a lot of money on them.

A girl cares much more about what you say to her, how you say it, and the special way you show her attention and treat her than she does about where you take her.

At times you will spend money on her, maybe a lot of money. But don't think that to make her feel special you always have to spend money.

A third reason dating is in a rut is because of fear. Guys do the same old things for fear of something going wrong. Guys think dating has so many risks to begin with, why take any unnecessary chances on a creative date?

True, risks go along with varying from the norm, but great rewards also result. The girl will see how much time and effort you have put into planning a good time and she will appreciate it. She will know that you aren't taking her for granted. She will enjoy the date more, too. Planning a creative date will enhance your reputation. Your date will spread the word to others about how creative you are and how much fun you are.

Fourth, guys can get lazy. You don't have to spend much time thinking out the date if you know you're going to a movie and dinner. It's only a question of which movie and what restaurant.

Fifth and finally, guys just don't know what to do on a date. That's where this chapter will help you. Read on for some ideas that should stir your creativity.

CREATIVE GENIUS

To give you an idea of the lengths to which you can go, listen as a creative genius at dating explains one of his dates:

> I wanted to show my girlfriend that I really thought she was special, so I planned a spectacular date. To help me pull it off, I asked a friend to help. He can imitate an impeccable British accent which I figured would add to the flavor of the night.

We scouted out a secluded spot in a state park to eat, at the foot of a mountain beside a small pond, surrounded on three sides by trees and flowers. We made a table with concrete blocks and plywood, then put a table cloth over the wood with a lace table cloth on top of it. The table held a kerosene lamp, a vase of flowers, salt and pepper. We had large cushions to sit on, and a hibachi grill for cooking. We had a portable stereo to play piano music during dinner.

Several logistical problems still needed attention. One was the delivery of sparkling grape juice. An attendant at the train station in the park agreed to keep the glasses and juice chilled for us. She even offered to carry them to us on a tray at the prescribed time.

When a park ranger drove by, he offered to help us, especially with the adventure I wanted to take after dinner. He wrote fifteen clues that my date and I would have to figure out to lead us to the final destination. We decided that he would hand us the first clue, but in an unusual way. With everything nearly ready, I left to change clothes and pick up my date. I told my date nothing, only to wear tennis shoes and bring her Bible, so she had no idea what was going on. Fortunately, her parents trusted me.

When we pulled up in the parking lot, I suggested that we walk around a bit before eating. It was a perfect evening, clear and cool with a soft breeze.

As we were walking in front of the mountain, a fourteen-year-old guy walked over, dressed in a tux with a dinner towel draped over one arm and two menus in his hand. He asked, in his British accent, "I say, Sir, would you and your lady like to dine at the Restaurant of the Rock?" My date looked at me and said, "What's going on?" I shrugged and suggested we try it.

Then my friend took a flower out of his coat pocket and asked, "May I pin a flower on your lady, Sir?" and pinned the little corsage on her. Then he escorted us over to the table.

We had made the menus out of cardboard. They were blue with red ribbons tied on them and "Restaurant of the . . ." was written in the corner and a piece of granite rock was below the lettering. At the bottom was a picture of the mountain.

Inside it read, *Restaurant of the Rock — Dinner Menu.* The

entrees listed were German Grits (potato salad), Canadian Kernels (corn on the cob), Peruvian Pits (fresh sliced peaches), Korean Cow (teriyaki steak), Greek Goose Juice (sparkling grape juice) and Texarkana Tea (iced tea).

About that time our "waiter" walked up with an appetizer platter covered by glass. The appetizers were sliced tomatoes, a pile of them. My date's father had an acre of tomato plants behind their home, so they had them coming out of their ears, and she hated tomatoes. The waiter put two slices on my plate and then put the rest in front of her. She nearly rolled off her cushion with laughter.

After our waiter had served dinner, the lady from the train station came over with the sparkling grape juice. She had changed clothes and was now dressed to the hilt. Where she got the outfit, I'll never know!

She brought the juice over and handed it to our waiter and set the glasses on the table. The waiter put in a corkscrew, pulled out the cork, showed me the bottle, showed my date the bottle, and put a little bit in my glass so I could taste it.

When we finished dinner our waiter brought us a finger bowl to wash our hands. As we got up to leave, the crowd that had gathered to watch began to clap.

Just then, my park ranger friend drove up in his patrol car. He slammed on the brakes, jumped out of the car and started talking on his walkie-talkie as he came toward us.

Our waiter began smart-mouthing the ranger and drew him into a royal argument. My date didn't know what to think. The ranger finally said, "Look kid, you give me any more trouble, and I'm going to throw all of you out of here."

The ranger pretended to write me a ticket, but instead he was writing down the first clue of our adventure. It read, *You are about to begin an adventure. Every clue will be contained in the Bible. Go to the train station and ask the conductor for the next clue.*

Off we went. The conductor's clue read, *Where there is no vision the people perish.* We looked and looked until we saw a viewfinder. When we peered into it, we found the next clue written on a note in front of the lens. It read, *A light set on a hill cannot be hidden.* As we searched we saw a candle on top of a large rock nearby. Under the candle the next clue read *There was no room at the inn.* So we went to the park hotel for the next clue. This went on for fifteen clues. The final clue led us to a large bell tower overlooking the lake. My friend had left us the stereo and some soft drinks. We laughed the rest of the evening.

What a creative date!

This date is not for beginners. It took a lot of preparation and coordination, but it should inspire you to start where you are and begin making your dates more creative.

MEGA IDEAS

The number of ideas for dates is almost infinite; you should rarely have to do the same thing twice.

Planning is the key. Proverbs 21:5 says, "The plans of the diligent surely lead to advantage." Use these steps as you plan your date.

● Think creatively as you look at some of the different ideas for dates.

● Choose from different types of dates depending on the occasion, mood and personal preferences of your date. Familiarize yourself with each group of dates listed below.

● Plan practical steps to accomplish the dates. Get a pen and paper ready to brainstorm your plans.

Sports Dates

golf	bowling
basketball	roller skating
tennis	ice skating
miniature golf	waterskiing
croquet	snowskiing
racketball	jogging
badminton	swimming
horseshoes	ping pong
pool/bumper pool	frisbee

walking

Advantages:
- — Fun
- — Exercise
- — Can involve others
- — Usually inexpensive

Disadvantages:
- — Your date might not be interested in sports
- — Your date could hurt your ego by beating you!
- — You could get too competitive
- — Your date could get injured

A Creative Touch:

Have your date ride her bicycle while you run. Afterward, go for something to drink while you cool down.

Outdoor Dates

Go boating
  canoeing
  sailing
  rafting
  sightseeing
  hiking
  fishing
  mountain climbing
  bicycling
  horseback riding
  on a picnic
Fly kites

Build sand castles
Visit amusement parks
  zoos
  wildlife sanctuaries
  outdoor gardens
  state parks
Take a country drive
  nature/wildlife photos
Watch sunrise/sunset
Collect seashells, leaves
Have a cookout
Play shuffleboard

Walk on the beach, in woods, along streets

Advantages:
- — New experience
- — Suntan in summer

Disadvantages:
- — Change in weather
- — Sometimes must travel a distance
- — Bugs

A Creative Touch:
        Pick your date up early. Take your date to a place to watch the sunrise. Afterwards, go for breakfast.

Crazy Dates
        Go to a fair
        Go for a hay ride
        Go for an airplane ride
        Go on a double date with parents (TRY IT!)
        Go on a group date in a convertible
        Have a water pistol fight
        Have a water balloon fight
        Learn to drive a stick shift
        Make a video
        Plant a garden
        Dress up (like the '50s) and get photographed
        Have scavenger hunts with a polaroid camera or a tape
            recorder (have two couples think up items for one
            another to look for)
Advantages:
        — Memorable
        — Creative
        — Fun
        — Can involve others
Disadvantages:
        — Potential to be a flop
        — Some people might think you are weird
A Creative Touch:
        Kidnap your date and take her on a long ride. End up at a studio where you can get photographed in Old West costumes. Let her parents in on your plans ahead of time.

Inexpensive Dates
        Go to library   Play TV video games
        Go to a playground   Play table games
        Go get ice cream   Play hide and seek

Go get a Coke and talk
Go to pet shop
Go caroling
Go window shopping
Go for walks
Build something
    (models, etc.)
Build snowman
Babysit
Look at Christmas lights
Put a puzzle together
Walk around mall
Look through old pictures
Play charades with friends

Play the guitar
Make candy
Make popcorn
Make ice cream
Study
Sing together

Bake cookies
Wash her dog
Watch home movies
Have snowball fight
Roast marshmallows
Fly paper airplanes

Ride the city's transit to park, zoo, etc., or just around for a while

Advantages:
— Don't have to have money
— Fun
— Variety

Disadvantages:
— Potential to never treat your date "extra special"

A Creative Touch:
Plan with your date how the two of you can go out for less than one dollar and go no more than one mile from her house. Do it that night.

Performing Arts Dates

Opera
Ballet
Musicals
Museums
Art Festivals

Plays
Orchestra
Dinner Theaters
Concerts
Craft Shows

Advantages:
— Learning experience
— Variety

— Can go with groups
Disadvantages:
— Some have little opportunity to talk
A Creative Touch:
Go to a play. Afterward, go for a stroll and discuss the plot together. Decide what the playwright wanted to communicate.

Ministry Dates

Visit convalescent centers
   orphanages
   juvenile homes
   sick friends
   hospitals
Have a Bible study with friends
Treat another couple
Take cookies to a friend
Pass out tracts
Wash your youth minister's car
Babysit your Sunday school teacher's children
Advantages:
— Eternal results
— Satisfaction of serving
Disadvantages:
— Potential for rejection
A Creative Touch:
Take a non-Christian couple out to an amusement park. Afterward, share how each of you accepted Christ. Ask if they have ever had a similar experience. Explain how they can. Give them an opportunity to accept Christ or call you if they want to talk about it more.

Dinner Dates

Have a cookout
Have progressive dinners with friends
Try different countries each week (for example: Japa-

nese, Mexican, Italian dinners)
Guy fix the dinner
Go to breakfast together
Go to a specialty restaurant

Advantages:
— Shows her how special she is
— Good for celebrating important occasions
— Lots of conversation
— Learn different cultures

Disadvantages:
— Expensive
— Must know which fork to use

A Creative Touch:
Go to a restaurant and each of you order something that you haven't tried before.

Spectator Dates

Movies   Circus
Rodeo
Athletic event (football, basketball, tennis, golf, baseball, etc.)

Advantages:
— Enjoyable
— Can take a lot of friends

Disadvantages:
— Not always able to maximize communication

A Creative Touch:
Go to an athletic event with a large group. Afterward, see if you can get the team to sign autographs.

PUTTING A DATE TOGETHER

With all the varied options to choose from, you may be confused even now. "With so much to do, what do we do first?" Here are some practical tips on how to know which date to pick.

Determine her likes. What interests her the most? Does

she like the outdoors or the performing arts? Eliminate those things she does not like.

Count your money. This will often narrow down the choices. If you do have a lot of money, spend it wisely.

Maximize conversation. One of the main reasons for dating is to grow in your friendship. Always try to structure as much time to talk as possible.

Insure a fun time. Take time to thoroughly plan your dates. Go over all the details. Plan fun dates. The more the girl enjoys the time, the longer she will remember it.

Keep dates out of the rut. Try not to plan the same date twice. When it's a hit, do it again, but later. Keep track of what you have done before. Add variety. Combine different kinds of dates for even more options to choose from. For example, pick a crazy date after a dinner date.

Include others. Group dating helps take the pressure off keeping the conversation going. In addition, you build other relationships, and it keeps you out of tempting situations.

Pick different times. Plan dates for morning and afternoon as well as in the evening.

Avoid tempting situations. Avoid places or people that put compromising thoughts in your head, especially movies, videos, plays, anything with suggestive material in it. Your date is special not only to you but also to God and her parents, so take good care of her.

Pick one. If you still haven't selected a date, close your eyes and point to one. Regardless of which one it is, it will be a great one.

ACTION SECTION

1. Come up with five creative dates.

   (1) _____

_____

   (2) _____

_____

   (3) _____

(4) _____

(5) _____

2. Plan a date for less than $3 and within ten miles from your home that would last at least two hours. Write it down here: _____
_____
_____

3. Write down what happened when you completed one of these dates. _____
_____
_____

4. Memorize Proverbs 21:5.

8

Waiting Creatively (Girls Only) ♥

HAVE you ever counted the times you've looked at the phone, hoping a guy would call to ask you out? Waiting to date can be nerve-racking. Since guys initiate dates, they choose whether to date or not. But girls are stuck by the phone, waiting, biting their nails and hoping.

And not dating can eat away at a girl's self-image. Thoughts and feelings get out of control.

The logic goes like this: "Other girls get dates, so what's wrong with me? I use deodorant and wash my hair, my clothes are clean, so it must be me. Something's wrong with me. I'm ugly, stupid, boring. . . That's it! Nobody likes me, so of course they won't go out with me. They probably hate me, but just pretend they don't. Nobody likes me. I'm weird. Oh, I'm just worthless."

And waiting is depressing.

You think . . . "I'll never get married."

And then . . . "My life is being wasted."

And you conclude . . . "I'll do anything to get a date."
And you already know from chapter 6 where this leads.

DOWN IN THE DUMPS

You know you shouldn't think like this, but that really doesn't help much. To help you better understand your feelings and how you can work your way out of them, let's look at each of those negative thoughts.

"Nobody likes me." The first thought goes like this: *Everybody is dating. That is, everybody but me. Since I'm not going out, it must mean that nobody likes me. Everybody hates me. I feel like eating worms.*

This is wrong thinking. First, you might be exaggerating. Surely *someone* likes you. But even if all your friends reject you, God loves you. He proved that love when His Son died for you. Now you are His child and He wants to take care of you and express His love to you. Jesus Christ knows how it feels to be rejected by everyone — read Luke 4:28,29 (that's pretty heavy rejection). So you can talk with Him about how you feel.

When you begin feeling like nobody likes you, do these things. First, consider how much God loves you. Read passages in the Bible that assure you of this, such as Romans 5:1-8. Second, write down the names of three people you know love you. Third, go to a quiet place and express your feelings to Jesus. He loves you and wants to help you feel loved. He knows how you feel, so trust Him to help you.

"I'm worthless." Thoughts like this one are very common when girls wait to date. The reasoning is: *I'm not good enough for anybody to date. I'm dumb and ugly. I'm a real loser. I'm worthless.*

The truth is that you are valuable and important. Your worth as an individual is not based on whether or not you date. Your worth is based on the *fact* that God loves you. God created you and gave you a unique personality. He made you just the way you are and put you in just the place you are. When you wonder if you are worthwhile, read Psalm 139 and write down seven reasons from that passage in the Bible why you are special.

"My life is being wasted." The reasoning behind this thought is: *My life is going down the tubes. I don't have a boyfriend. What is life if I don't have anyone to love?*

Your life is definitely not being wasted when you aren't dating. This is valuable time in which you can learn and grow by spending time with Christ and others like never again. You have the opportunity to build deep, lasting friendships with other girls and to get involved in extensive ministry projects, even to build your relationship with your parents, brothers and sisters.

"I'll do anything to get a date." After a while, you panic and start thinking of every possible way you can get a date. You've reached the point where you're ready to call a guy and beg him to go out with you. You're so impatient that you are willing to get physically involved if that's what it takes.

What can you do? You need to focus on trusting God. He knows what's best for you and at the right time He will provide a date for you.

"I'm weird." Soon you begin thinking that you have to wait because you are weird. You figure, *Guys must think I'm strange, so they don't ask me out.*

These kinds of thoughts cause you either to withdraw or to act crazy. Whenever you have thoughts like these, stop and remember that you are not weird. Everyone is different and unique, and God has made you just like you are. If you aren't dating, God must have a reason for it. Just be yourself.

"I'll never get married." Of all the negative thoughts, this is the most depressing. You may think, *I can't marry unless I date, and since I'm not dating, I'll never get married. I'll be an old maid. I'll be lonely the rest of my life.*

The truth is that God has someone already picked out for you, assuming He wants you to marry. Since He has that person picked out, you don't have to worry. Instead of worrying, use this time to pray for your future husband.

BE THE BEST

If you want to date the best, then you must be the best. Focus on preparing yourself for that special man God will one day bring into your life.

It takes time. You will not change overnight, so start now to be the woman God wants you to be.

One girl did. At one time in her life she didn't have a date for more than a year. But after that waiting time, she wrote this letter:

I knew if I wanted to marry a special guy, I needed to become the kind of girl he would be attracted to. I knew I could catch most any guy with sex, but if I wanted to attract the man God made for me, then I'd have to have the qualities God thinks are important. So I worked on developing godly qualities.

I knew that looks don't last, so I wanted to develop my personality.

It wasn't always the easy way. But instead of feeling sorry for myself or figuring out how to get dates, I began to develop friendships with other girls. I stopped worrying about myself and helped these new friends.

The time and effort paid off. After a whole year of waiting, I started to date a terrific guy. We eventually married, and now he treats me with such care. God has given me someone who is wonderful.

INTRODUCING RUBY

You need to be God's best, but what does that really mean? Going to finishing school? Reading etiquette books? Reading Wonder Woman comic books? What kind of woman does God want you to be?

Be like Ruby. Ruby is a woman in the Bible. She's called Ruby, because one translation of the Bible tells us "Her worth is far above rubies."

You can read about Ruby in Proverbs 31:10-31. Each verse describes a different characteristic of an excellent wife. Consider how you can build these characteristics of an excellent wife into your life while you are waiting. Then, when God brings that special guy into your life, you will know how to be God's best for him.

Terrific Teammate

"The heart of her husband trusts in her, And he will have no lack of gain. She does him good and not evil all the days of her life" (verses 11,12).

Ruby's husband knew he could count on her because she wanted to do him good. She was considerate, not selfish. She put him second only to God.

Projects to develop consideration:

— Look for the needs of your friends and family and serve at least one person each day.

— Do a project around the house without your parents asking you.

Cheerful Worker

"She looks for wool and flax, and works with her hands in delight" (verse 13).

Ruby worked with delight. She was cheerful. She had a positive attitude toward her responsibilities.

Projects to develop cheerfulness:

— Do not grumble or complain when you are asked to do something, but learn to smile and ask for anything else that needs to be done.

— Picture yourself as working for Christ, and sing songs to Him while you work.

Great Cook

"She is like merchant ships;

Ruby knew how to shop and cook.

She brings her food from afar.
She rises also while it is
still night and gives food to
her household, and portions to
her maidens (verses 14,15).

(Girls, to some guys this is a
priority!)

Projects to learn to shop and cook:
— Go shopping with your mother, and learn to look for sales, compare prices and use coupons.
— Once a month, fix dinner for the family by yourself.

Business Woman

"She considers a field and
buys it; from her earnings she
plants a vineyard" (verse 16).

Ruby knew how to make and
manage money. If something
ever happened to her husband,
she could provide for her family.

Projects to learn to manage money:
— Take classes in school that will best prepare you for a career.
— Be wise with your money by giving the first 10 percent of your money to the Lord, praying before buying anything, waiting for sales, and saving some money each month.

Exercise Enthusiast

"She girds herself with
strength, and makes her arms
strong" (verse 17).

Ruby was a physical fitness
enthusiast. She kept her body
in shape.

Projects to get in shape physically:
— Take up a recreational sport, or get into an aerobics class.
— Get plenty of sleep, do calisthenics, and eat healthy meals.

Creative Genius

"She senses that her gain is good; her lamp does not go out at night. She stretches out her hands to the distaff, and her hands grasp the spindle" *(verses 18,19).*

Ruby used her time wisely by learning how to enhance the beauty of her home.

Projects to learn home decoration:
— Take classes, read books, or ask others to help you learn cross stitch, needlepoint, pottery, painting.
— Decorate your home during different holidays and seasons.

Minister to People

"She extends her hand to the poor; and she stretches out her hands to the needy" *(verse 20).*

Ruby felt compassion for the poor and needy. And she did something about it.

Projects to minister:
— Get involved in a ministry at your church such as leading a Bible study, discipling a younger girl, or helping in a children's ministry.
— Minister at school by befriending a lonely person, talking to non-Christians about Christ, writing notes of encouragement.

Fashionable Dresser.

"She is not afraid of the snow for her household, for all her household are clothed with scarlet. She makes coverings for herself; her clothing is fine linen and purple" *(verses 21,22).*

Ruby was fashionable but frugal. She not only knew how to buy clothes properly, but she could make them as well.

Projects to learn to buy and make clothes wisely:
— Don't get hung up on name brands, but balance quality with price.
— Have your mother or a friend show you how to sew. Practice mending or making a dress by yourself.

Look at what happened because Ruby took time to develop herself. Verse 28 says "Her children rise up and bless her; her husband also, and he praises her, 'Many daughters have done nobly, but you excel them all.' " Ruby's children and husband thought highly of her. Her children praised her and thought she was the greatest. Her husband also praised her. He said that of all the women who had succeeded as a great wife and mother she was the best of all. How would you like for your children and husband to think this way of you?

Over the next five months, memorize Proverbs 31:10-31 by learning one verse each week. As you memorize, make Ruby your guiding model that week and seek to imitate her.

TEST TIME

To help you determine what you need to do to become like Ruby, take the following test. Rate yourself 1-10.

1. You serve needs that your family and friends have (verses 11,12).   _____
2. You do not grumble or complain when given work to do (verse 13).   _____
3. You are a wise grocery shopper and good cook (verses 14,15).   _____
4. You manage your money wisely (verse 16).   _____
5. You are in good physical shape (verse 17).   _____
6. You decorate your home on different occasions (verses 18,19).   _____
7. You minister to the needy and lonely at school and at church (verse 20).   _____
8. You buy clothes wisely (verses 21,22).

Total score _____ ÷ 8 = _____ Rating

DON'T JUMP THE GUN

Well, how did you do on the test? Did you find some areas to work on? If you did, think through which of the areas listed you want to work on first.

The main thing is to take advantage of this waiting time. Use it to improve yourself in every area — mentally, physically, emotionally and spiritually. Don't look at this time as wasted time or an opportunity missed. Take advantage of this time to prepare yourself for that special man. It is much harder to start after you marry. This is valuable time you will never have again.

Because this is such valuable time, be *willing* to wait. It is easy to become impatient and go out manhunting. Don't jump the gun. One day he will tell you how much he appreciates you being like Ruby.

A PRAYER OF DEDICATION

You may have resented this waiting time. Many young women do. The following is a prayer you can pray to receive this time as a God-given opportunity to prepare you for that special guy.

Dear Lord Jesus, I'm sorry for getting upset for having to wait to date. I now see that You have given me this time to prepare me for that special guy You have picked out for me. I was wrong for resenting my situation. Please forgive me.

Lord Jesus, thank You for this time of preparation. I receive it from You. I commit myself to make the most of this waiting time. I want to be the best, not only for my future husband, but also for You. I love You, Lord. In Your name, Amen.

ACTION SECTION

1. Write down any negative thoughts you have had while waiting. _____

_____

2. Confess each one specifically to God, asking for forgiveness.

3. What kind of wife do you want to be? _____
_____
_____

4. What do you think of Ruby? Why? _____
_____
_____

5. Name the three characteristics of Ruby that you need to work on the most.

(1) _____
(2) _____
(3) _____

6. Pick one of these characteristics and write how you plan to build it into your life. Be specific. Write down the steps you will take. _____
_____
_____

7. Write out a prayer thanking God for giving you this waiting time to become more like Ruby. _____
_____
_____
_____

8. Memorize Proverbs 31:29,30.

9

Keeping the Other Person Interested ♥

*J*EFF seemed to have all the basics of dating under control. He was "old enough" to date, knew how to pick a winner and was very creative in planning dates. One problem: He rarely could get a girl to go out with him more than once, no matter how hard he tried! Jeff, like a lot of students, couldn't keep a girl interested.

Although getting the first date is hard, sometimes getting the second and third dates are even harder. After the first date, the mystery is gone and the other person begins to discover what you are like. Even if you have mastered all the preliminaries, keeping a date interested in you can be difficult.

THE CLUES

The mystery of developing great relationships (dating relationships or otherwise) gets solved when the other person's needs are considered ahead of your own. In Philippians 2:3,4 you can find the clues to solving that mystery:

> Do nothing from selfishness or empty conceit, but with humility of mind let each of you regard one another as more important than himself.
> Do not merely look out for your own personal interest, but also for the interests of others.

Clue 1: Selfishness Stinks

Few things turn people off more quickly than bad odors.

Normally, Bill's wife greets him when he comes home from work. "She makes me feel special by the way she welcomes me home. When she hears the door open, she comes running to the door to hug me and smother me with kisses.

"But when I've eaten spicy Mexican food for lunch, by afternoon my breath can kill an elephant at thirty feet. Without warning, my wife comes running to the door with wide-open arms ready to kiss me. 'Honey! You're home!' I drop my briefcase and open my arms. Then it happens. She covers her nose and mouth and gags, 'Arggggh! What have you been eating?' Then she turns and runs in the opposite direction."

Selfishness is as attractive as bad breath. It stinks! Selfishness means looking out for only your own interests and not for the interests of others. This attitude says, "On my dates, I want to do what I want, when I want to do it, where I want to do it and it doesn't matter what my date wants." No one wants to be around a selfish person. Philippians 2:3 says, "Do nothing from selfishness." The first clue in relating to your date is to avoid selfishness at all costs.

Clue 2: Conceit Cuts

The rest of Philippians 2:3 tells us, "Do nothing from selfishness or empty conceit." A conceited person is stuck on his looks, abilities, or position. On a date, all this person wants to do is talk about himself.

A conceited person not only thinks he is the greatest, but he looks down on other people, even his date. He loudly expresses that his date is fortunate to go out with him. When his friends sense his attitude of conceit, they avoid him. They don't like to be around him. They develop a bad attitude toward him and try to "cut him down to size." The second clue causes the conceited person to be lonely and isolated. Avoid conceit.

Clue 3: Humility Helps

Humility, as Paul defines it in Philippians 2:3, means regarding others as more important than yourself — the opposite of conceit.

Humility comes out most in the way you treat your date. When you consider your date as more important than yourself, you want to treat him well. You do things that show him how important he is. Often, you do things that require time and effort because you know he is worth it.

When Bill and his wife Debby were dating, she made him a shirt for his birthday. One day Bill thought he could show her how important she was to him by making her a dress! At the time, he thought this was a great idea.

"I started by asking a friend to teach me how. First, we went to a fabric store and picked out an easy pattern. A sun dress was the simplest pattern I could buy. Just cut it out, sew one seam up the back, stitch on the straps, hem it, and it's done.

"Then we spent the entire day making the dress. My friend worked on a dress of hers and I followed her example. One thing I learned was that God did not create me to sew. Several times I almost sewed my fingers together. Twice the needle broke and hit me in the face.

"I accused my friend of intentionally making it hard on me, but she replied that any ten-year-old could do it.

"I was so frustrated that I didn't finish hemming it. My sweetheart had invited me over for dinner that night, so I put the unfinished dress in a box and took it with me.

"When I arrived, I gave her the dress and said, 'I made this for you. I hope you like it.' When she opened the box, she was delighted. She couldn't believe I had made it for her. She put it on and wore it all evening, even when we went for a walk. Since it wasn't hemmed, the bottom of the dress had strings hanging down from it. It looked awful! But she wore it. Not because of how it looked, but because I had made her feel important."

Humility makes your date feel special. So, if you want a relationship to continue, remember to act with humility.

Clue 4: Service Satisfies

Philippians 2:4 says you should look out for the interests of others, not "Number 1." Selfishness looks out for your interests, but service helps you put the interests of others before your own.

Serving expresses itself in the choices you make. When you serve, you will choose those things your date likes, not necessarily what you like — whether it is where to go, what to do, or when to leave.

Discovering these four clues will continue to attract your date more than anything else. Once he or she gets to know you, that person will continue to want to get to know you more. You may be cute, fun, or have lots of money, but if your date feels like you don't care about him, he won't stick around for long.

SECRETS FOR SUCCESS (GUYS ONLY)

Now let's look at some secrets that will help guys carry out the clues, and solve the mystery of keeping a girl interested.

Guys, what are the secrets that show that you put the girl's needs first?

Manners

People have written about manners for centuries. One article, "A History of Dating," reads:

In the sixteenth century, a gentleman of Renaissance Italy was cautioned against using bad language in mixed company, wearing a toothpick around his neck, scratching himself in immodest places and looking in his handkerchief after blowing his nose as if pearls and rubies had fallen from his brain.[1]

Today, as well as in the sixteenth century, you need manners. Be a gentleman to your date.

● Let us emphasize again, that you need to ask her out at least three days in advance. Never call up and ask a girl out, then say, "Great, I'll be over in a half hour." Ask her out in advance to show her that you think time with her is important, and so she won't think you take her for granted or that she was a last-minute idea. If she is a last-minute idea, wait and ask her out for next week.

● Plan your dates. Knowing what you will do every minute keeps your date exciting . . . and keeps you out of trouble.

● Pick her up on time. Don't be late, like the next day. And don't be too early, like the day before. If you arrive early, it means longer time to talk to the parents. If you're comfortable around them, go ahead. If not, drive around the block for a while.

● Go to the door to pick her up. Never blow your horn and then wait for her in your car. Talk about dangerous — that's dangerous! You risk having her dad come out to strangle you.

● Talk to her parents for a few minutes. Do this every date. Find out how they are doing. Tell them where you are going on the date. Tell them what time you plan to have their daughter home, and ask if they approve.

● Rise to recognize your date and/or her parents. If they enter the room when you are sitting, stand up politely.

● Open doors for her. Let her enter first. This includes car doors, house doors, restaurant doors, gym doors, classroom doors . . . any kind of doors. If she gets out before you have a chance, ask her if she will let you open the door for her in the future. But don't push her back and make her walk through again while you hold the door!

● Pull the chair out for her to sit down. But don't pull it out too far — she will think she is overweight, or she may miss it and hit the floor. Try not to huff and puff when you push it back in or wipe the sweat from your forehead after all the work you did pushing her back to the table.

● Walk on the side of the sidewalk closest to the street when walking together. This tradition resulted from the times potholes, mud puddles and garbage covered the roads. With the guy on the outside, he would get splashed if a vehicle came, but the girl would be protected. She will still feel protected if you do this. If you see that a car is about to splash you, just duck.

● Never talk about how much a date costs. Comments like, "Look at this check. I can't believe how much your meal cost!" should be avoided "at all costs."

● Never talk about your past relationships with other girls unless she asks. Nor should you compare your date to former girlfriends. For example, you wouldn't say, "This is the way Susie and I used to hold hands," or "Jenny always made us cookies to eat when we came to this park."

Do Special Things

If your date made a cake but left out the sweetener, it would taste terrible. In the same way, in dating you want to make sure you add sweetener by doing special things. In relationships, doing special things adds that touch of class that lets a girl know how much she means to you.

● Praise at least one Christ-like quality in her life every date. For example, compliment her sensitivity if she detects that a person is hurting emotionally.

● Send her a card and a flower. Offer no reason other than her specialness. Tell her you were thinking of her and wanted to brighten up her day.

● Ask if you can pray for her on the date. Pray for

any needs or problems she brought up while talking on the date. Take this opportunity to thank God for the privilege of spending time with her. Don't worry about how your prayer sounds. Your date will admire your desire to pray for her regardless of how you express yourself.

Build Her Security

● Do not allow her to place her security in her relationship with you. Encourage her to keep her focus on the Lord Jesus by encouraging her involvement in her church and youth group.

● Guard against talking about marriage. If you have dated for a while this can cause a girl's emotions to go berserk. Just the remote mention of marriage can build expectations. So avoid the topic. Do not talk about marriage until you can put a ring on her finger.

● Maintain your priorities. Do not devote all of your attention to your date. Set an example for her. Keep your time for Christ, your family, your church and your studies in the proper perspective. Your date will respect your lifestyle. And she will not feel smothered by you.

● Learn to relax. When you are at ease, your date will feel comfortable. Don't worry about things going wrong. Remember, guys, girls think you are the greatest.

● Be yourself. Don't pretend to be someone you're not. Sooner or later the real you will come out. If you haven't been yourself, then she will be in for a shock. Besides, now — not later — is the best time to find out if she likes you for who you really are.

SECRETS FOR SUCCESS (GIRLS ONLY)

How many times has a guy picked you up, taken you out, dropped you off at home, never to call you again? What a killer experience. If this has not happened to you — great! But if it has, the following suggestions may give you an idea of how to keep it from happening again. It all boils down to putting his needs first.

Admire Your Date

Your date needs you to look up to him. That shows you respect him. You're probably thinking, "That's the last thing he needs." You're partially right. Guys do not need their egos pumped up. Some have gotten their egos out of control already. They walk around with their chests out like they are macho. They stop any place they can see their reflection and say "ooh" and "aah," and "you handsome rascal."

No, your date doesn't need his ego blown up any more. But he does need for you to admire him. Note the difference. Ego pumping flatters him. It focuses on his physical appearance. Admiration builds up his inner qualities. Because people usually notice the physical, most guys concentrate on that. But if you will notice his inner qualities, then he will begin to concentrate on those.

As your date responds to life in a Christ-like way, he needs to know how much you admire him for it. Express it like this:

Tell him
- "I respect you because . . ."
- "Some of the qualities that I admire in you are . . ."
- "I'm proud of the way you . . ."

Write him
- "Here are leadership characteristics I see in your life . . ."
- "You make me feel secure by . . ."
- "The thing I admire about you most is . . ."

Show him
- Make a plaque with the different qualities you see in his life.
- Cross-stitch a verse of Scripture that reminds you of him.
- Buy a gift that expresses how highly you think of him. It doesn't have to be expensive, just appropriate.

Appreciate Your Date

Some girls forget to say "thank you," taking a special friend for granted. She expects him to take her out and treat her special, but she forgets that the guy worked a part-time job all week just to have the money to go out. Sure, you may say the usual "Thank you for tonight — I really enjoyed it." But if you want a guy to enjoy the time he spends with you, let him know how much you appreciate it.

Don't just thank him at the end of the date. Thank him during the date. Afterward, write him a thank-you card for his efforts. Do this only if you're sincere and want to encourage him to ask you out again.

This causes the guy to feel that he pleases you. He knows you are grateful for what he did to make sure you had a good time. He will notice this difference between you and others. Each date, pick one or two of the following ways to say "thank you":

- "I'm enjoying the time with you. You are fun."
- "I appreciate the way you make me feel special."
- "I wanted to thank you again for the date this weekend. It was great."
- Send a thank-you card.
- Send brownies or chocolate chip cookies with a note of thanks.

Abide

Guys scare easily. If they sense a "noose" tightening, they often run. Therefore, it is important to put your security in your relationship with Jesus Christ rather than in your relationship with a guy. The Bible calls this "abiding." Abiding means to trust Christ to take care of your needs and not focus on the relationship to meet those needs. You cease to abide when you begin to have thoughts like: "How does he feel about me? What's going on in his relationships with other girls? Why didn't he call me today?"

To keep your security in Christ, check yourself frequently on these:

● Spend time alone with God daily. Talk to Him about things other than your dating relationships.

● Ask an older Christian woman to guide you. Guidance will help you keep proper perspective.

● Look for the warning signs — such as jealousy, possessiveness, and insecurity.

● Be careful about your emotions. Continually ask God to keep them from taking over.

● Guard against expectations. When you start expecting him to call, come over, or ask you out, then you have set yourself up for disappointment.

CAUTION! DON'T GO OVERBOARD ON ANY OF THESE. JUST DO WHAT'S APPROPRIATE.

ACTION SECTION

Guys Only

1. Think of the last time you took a girl out. Place a check mark under the appropriate answer to each item.

	Needs work	Doing Fine
Asked out in advance		
Date planned		
Arrived on time		
Picked up at door		
Talked with parents		
Rose when she entered		
Opened doors		
Pulled out chairs for her		
Walked on the outside edge		
Didn't talk about costs		
Praised Christ-like qualities		
Sent cards and flowers		
Prayed for her		
Kept her and my security in Jesus		
Didn't talk about marriage		
Maintained my priorities		

Was relaxed
Acted like myself

2. Based on the above test, what three steps will you take to improve for your next date?

    (1) _____
    (2) _____
    (3) _____

Girls Only

1. In order to keep a guy interested, it helps to express admiration and appreciation for him and to abide in Christ by keeping your security in Him. Check yourself with this quiz and see how you are doing.

	Needs Work	Doing Fine
Expressed admiration		
Expressed appreciation		
Kept my security in Christ		

2. What area needs the most work? _____
_____

3. What three steps will you take to put this into practice?

    (1) _____
    (2) _____
    (3) _____

Guys and Girls

Memorize Philippians 2:3,4.

10

Going Together ♥

*B*ILL'S first steady girlfriend went out with him every Sunday. "Although we did the same thing every date, you will have to admit it was very creative. We sat on our potty chairs, watched TV and talked. I was three years old, and my girlfriend was two.

"Over the years, I have discovered that many things I learned when I was three are still true for students today. One of them is that students go through several different stages that lead to dating only one person."

STAGES TO SERIOUS DATING

1. *Group Dating.* A couple starts out dating with several other people. They go out with a whole group of friends and may or may not be paired off. But soon they discover each other and enjoy being together.

Dating in groups has several pluses. First, you build

relationships with many people, not just one. Second, if you have trouble making conversation with a date, group dating takes the pressure off. You can listen while others in the group talk. Third, dating in groups keeps you out of situations where you might give in to physical temptation.

2. *Couple Dating.* This is what everyone thinks of when you mention dating: a guy and girl go out alone. It may be a one-time date, or they may date occasionally. However, neither one is committed only to the other. If they date fairly often, they date other people as well. This is the healthiest stage of dating, because a person builds friendships with many different people. It's healthy also because there is no pressure from another person physically or emotionally. The person benefits by learning how to build good friendships with the opposite sex, yet avoids the problems of relationships advancing too fast.

3. *Consistent Dating.* After a couple has gotten to know each other, if they enjoy one another and have fun being together, they begin to date regularly. Each may occasionally go out with someone else, because no commitment has been made to date each other only.

4. *Commitment Dating.* In this stage, the couple dates no one else because they have made a commitment to date only each other. They may or may not have talked about their commitment. Either way, both understand that they will not pursue a relationship with another guy or girl.

Problems arise, though, if this commitment is not a mutual understanding. You're waltzing along, thinking everything is great . . . until one of you goes out with someone else. Then the old date hunts you down and jumps all over you. You have no idea why he's so angry. You thought you were going out without commitment, but he thought you were committed to each other.

This stage, commonly called "going together" or "going steady," has advantages and disadvantages. Have you ever wondered, should you or shouldn't you "go steady"?

GOING STEADY — GOOD OR BAD?

A Few of the Pluses of Commitment Dating . . .

1. *You no longer have to worry about getting a date.* Now you have someone to go out with you. No more trying to figure out who to ask. No more fear about being turned down. No more concern about being lonely or staying at home again on the weekend.

2. *You find it easier to be yourself.* You know the person accepts you so there's no need to be super careful about what you say or how you act. You can relax.

3. *You develop a deeper friendship.* Because you spend a lot of time with your steady, you get to know each other. You have someone with whom you can really talk. The special times together produce lasting memories.

4. *You learn to be more considerate.* Since you are so close, many of your choices and actions affect the other person, and you have to be more conscious of the needs of your date. You learn how to give up your desires and learn how to meet the other person's needs. You become more sensitive, understanding and considerate.

. . . And the Minuses

With these advantages, disadvantages are evident also. Remember, just because two people are going together doesn't mean they have these problems. There are potential disadvantages because of the tendency for relationships at this stage to head toward problems. If you are contemplating going together, think these through at first, so you will know what to guard against.

1. *You limit other friendships.* You wouldn't have as much time for your old friends and your ability to make new friends would be limited. Any free time you had you would spend with your old friends just to keep from losing touch.

2. *You tend to become possessive.* Many couples who go together complain of feeling tied down. A girl might get jealous if the guy talks to another girl. An attitude of ownership

develops. Mistrust, hurt and jealousy begin if every minute isn't spent together. This tends to produce frustration in the relationship.

3. *You tend to get more physically involved.* For most couples, it starts out with holding hands for a thrill. But after a while that gets old. Then they play "huggy bear." The thrill returns! But, that gets old, too. Then it's kissing . . . and more and more kissing, until the thrill is gone and all you have is foggy car windows.

4. *You can replace Jesus Christ with your new love.* Before going steady, all of your decisions center around Jesus and how your choices affect your relationship with Him. Afterward you make decisions on how they affect your sweetheart. Before, you looked to the Lord Jesus to meet your needs. This doesn't happen in every case, but before long your relationship with Christ could grow cold.

5. *You are limited in who you can date.* That's pretty obvious. You are committed, so you no longer have the freedom to go out with others. This can create problems if a holy hunk or spiritual fox arrives on the scene.

6. *You open yourself up for hurt.* In all relationships you can get hurt, but this is true especially in a dating relationship. Because of the emotional involvement, breaking up becomes difficult, even if you know the relationship isn't what God wants.

7. *You tend to take each other for granted.* The little things begin to disappear — like writing notes, making cookies, buying flowers, special dates, being patient, showing respect. Disagreements lead to arguments and conflict becomes a common experience.

8. *You can hinder each other's growth.* Growth comes from exposure to many new people and situations.

You should seriously consider all the negatives of commitment dating. It often takes the life out of a dynamic friendship and limits students before they're really able to make a choice based on long-term experience. For example, you may be totally satisfied eating vanilla ice cream because that's all you've ever tasted. Little do you realize that there are hundreds of flavors and all of them are good. If you tasted them all, vanilla might be your least favorite. In relationships, the more people you are around, the more you broaden your understanding of men and women. If you only date one person, your experience is limited.

BEHIND THE POPULARITY

Why do so many people want to date just one person, especially when the disadvantages are many? By far the greatest motivation is insecurity.

Security comes from feeling confident. It happens by knowing that your life is founded on something solid, immovable. The only secure people are those who have built their lives on the foundation of Jesus Christ. He is solid rock.

People whose lives aren't built on Jesus Christ don't have a solid foundation. Therefore, they are insecure. They lack confidence and assurance. Because of this, they look constantly for someone or something to meet this need.

They might put their security in *possessions*. They work jobs after school to make more money. They buy cars, clothes, stereos, and jewelry.

They might put their security in *position*. They have to lead everything. They want popularity. Their name has to be recognized.

They might put their security in *people*. They build their lives around relationships. For this reason many people want to go steady with just one person. Going with someone keeps down insecure feelings.

Unfortunately, possessions, positions, or people never solve the insecurity problem because they are temporary. Only Jesus Christ is permanent. The eternal Son of God is the only one who will never leave you nor forsake you (Hebrews 13:5). You can lose your possessions, your popularity and your relationships, but Christ sticks with you always (Matthew 28:20).

How can you know where you have put your security? To know, ask yourself the following questions:

- Do you always wonder if he or she still likes you?
- Do you panic when your steady talks with someone else?
- Do you compare yourself or your date to others to see if you measure up?
- Do you fall apart if he or she doesn't call?
- Do you wonder a lot about why your steady said or did a particular thing?
- Are you self-conscious about how you look?
- Do you cling to him, afraid to let him out of your sight?
- Does your life revolve around your steady?
- Are you comfortable only when you are doing things together?
- Do you tend to be by yourselves a lot?
- Does he easily upset you?
- Do you worry a lot about losing him?

If you have or ever will say "yes" to any of these questions, then read on. When you are insecure in your dating you suffer several consequences. For starters, neither person enjoys the relationship to the fullest. Neither can you enjoy other relationships. You always fear losing each other.

Insecurity comes from not trusting Jesus Christ to provide the best for you. You feel you must get it yourself. This leads to scheming and manipulating in the relationship. You try to control the relationship to make your steady meet your needs.

A SECURE RELATIONSHIP

When you place your security in Jesus Christ and not your date, you begin to overcome your insecurity. Then, with security, you have the ability to meet the other person's real needs. Here are some ways you can build a secure relationship:

1. *Don't ask yourself: "Is this the one?"* This gets your focus off the present and on the future. The time will come soon enough to consider the potential of marriage. Be careful

not to think about marriage too soon.

2. *Pray together.* This keeps both of you focused on the Lord. This will remind you around whom your relationship revolves. You can pray at the beginning or end of your date — or both.

3. *Keep your conversation away from the romantic.* This opens the door for your emotions and body to get out of control. For example, always talking about how much you love each other, how you are meant for each other or the possibility of marriage creates all kinds of temptations.

4. *Free your date to talk to others.* Allow each other to spend time with people. You may worry or be upset at first, but give each other space.

5. *Pray when you are anxious.* When questions like "What does he think of me?" or "Why is she talking to that guy?" bombard your mind, pray. Learn to take your worries to Christ and leave them with Him. Pray every time you feel anxious.

6. *Look to Christ to meet your needs.* To avoid scheming and manipulating to get your date to meet your needs, spend time daily with Jesus, reading the Bible, praying and meditating on the Scripture.

KNOWING WHEN IT'S RIGHT

Insecurity is wrong, so when is it all right to commit yourself to dating just one person? How can you know if commitment dating is the thing to do? 1 Corinthians 7:35 provides direction.

And this I say for your own benefit; not to put restraint upon you, but to promote what is seemly, and to secure undistracted devotion to the Lord (NIV).

This verse follows several verses on whether a person should marry. Commitment dating is not the same as being married, but there are many similarities. In fact, commitment dating often leads to marriage.

Scripture warns that when two people get married, it is harder for them to completely devote themselves to the Lord Jesus Christ. Because they need to care for one another, they can't spend as much time on their relationship with Christ.

This also happens when two people commit to going with each other. The desire to please your sweetheart consumes so much time and energy that your personal relationship with Jesus Christ suffers. A girl wrote:

> I had never even imagined that he would ask me out! Our relationship began terrifically. We both were committed Christians who were seeking God's will in our lives. I continued to date others, but knew that I was "falling fast!" He liked me a great deal too, but I held him at an arm's length for a long time for fear of commitment and having to be vulnerable to someone.
>
> We were apart for the summer. But in the fall we began dating again. I was ready and willing to let myself grow deeper in love. I guess it was at about this point that we started leaving God out of our relationship. We still prayed and went to church. But I got so caught up in my emotions. As I began to live for him, I drifted farther and farther from God.
>
> He, too, got caught up in his feelings for me and my constant outpouring of affection for him. We both got so totally wrapped up in each other that we began to argue and fight and demand things of each other. We knew where we could stab each other, and would battle constantly in a totally selfish way to get what we wanted. This built up over a period of about eight months. Both of us knew that something had to change. I suggested that we break up. His suggestion was to just "take the pressure off." Neither of us realized the real mistake. We needed Christ back as the center of our relationship.
>
> I am convinced that all of the problems we had in our relationship stemmed from our neglecting Christ.

YOUR TOP PRIORITY

Approach commitment dating with extreme caution, and only after extensive counsel with your parents. If they have any hesitations, respect that and, at the most, stay with consistent dating. When you focus so much of your attention and affection on your steady, then your commitment to Christ can suffer. Jesus Christ must have first place in your life. He can take second place to no one, not even a boyfriend or girlfriend. If you ever discover that you have dropped Him from first place in your life, or are in danger of doing so, you *must* do whatever it takes to put Him back in His rightful position — even if that means putting the relationship on hold for awhile.

The relationship must always encourage your relationship with Christ and never discourage it, so approach the decision of commitment dating very carefully. If you feel it would be for the right reason and would not hinder your walk with Christ, then go for it. But both of you should enter the relationship with the understanding that if commitment dating ever distracts from either person's commitment to Christ, then you will back off regardless of how much it may hurt.

Remember, steady dating is popular because it brings a sense of security. But this is among people who don't know the security of a relationship with Jesus Christ. That's why you shouldn't just assume that the popular way is the best way and that you should have a "steady." Go back to chapter 1. The purpose of dating is to build friendships; keep that clearly in mind.

CHECKLIST

The following checklist will help you determine whether Jesus Christ is in first place in your relationship with your boyfriend or girlfriend:

_____ I pray and read my Bible each day.

_____ I attend church weekly.

_____ I pray with my steady regularly.

_____ I am not physically involved with my steady.

_____ I continue to spend time with my other friends.

_____ My sweetheart and I talk freely and regularly about what God is doing in our lives.

_____ I obey my parents' desires concerning my dating.
_____ We minister to other people together and separately.
_____ We are open to God at any time to redirect (break off) our relationship.

WHERE TO NOW?

If you are going with someone, you may have seen areas in your relationship that need work after reading this chapter. Decide which area needs your attention. Your goal is to get things together the way they are supposed to be.

Area 1: Minor Problems. You can take care of them while still going together. You can solve these problems by merely refocusing your primary commitment onto Christ.

Area 2: Major Problems. Often the best way to handle these problems is to back off the commitment to date only each other. This gives you a chance to think and evaluate without your steady always around. You may or may not continue to date during this time. If you do continue to date, you don't date as often as before. You may decide to date others as well.

Area 3: Messed-up Relationship. You know that the only way to secure undivided devotion to Jesus Christ is to break up. This route is necessary especially if you have gotten involved physically. Because your thoughts, emotions, actions and habits get so out of control, the only hope of dealing with the impurity is to break up completely.

Too many times, students are involved in commitment dating before they are ready. This is a question that you need to approach at least as thoughtfully, prayerfully, and seriously as the decision to begin to date. So talk with God, talk with your parents, and carefully consider all the drawbacks of "going steady." If you believe it is right and your parents consent, then aim to make the relationship the very best — a growing friendship as you both focus yourselves on Christ.

ACTION SECTION

1. What stage of dating are you in right now?

_____

2. List the two biggest advantages of going together for you.
   (1) _____
   (2) _____

3. List the two biggest disadvantages of going together for you.
   (1) _____
   (2) _____

4. Do you struggle with placing your security in the people you date?

Yes   _____   No   _____
     Why? _____

_____

5. If you do, what steps will you take to overcome this?

_____
_____
_____

6. If you are going with someone, how would you rate the relationship? How would your parents?
_____   Right on target
_____   Close but not quite right
_____   Beginning to stray off course
_____   Headed in the wrong direction

7. What do you need to do to make the relationship what Jesus wants it to be?

_____
_____

8. Memorize 1 Corinthians 7:35.

11

Breaking Up ♥

AS a high school senior, Bill suffered the breakup of the century. He and his girlfriend had dated for four years, and everyone thought they were the perfect couple. She was captain of the cheerleaders and homecoming queen; he was president of the student body.

"One Saturday we had just started watching a sports program when my sweetheart asked if we could go for a walk. *What a terrible time to go for a walk,* I thought. So I suggested we do it later. But she insisted, so I gave in. It seemed like we walked for miles! The whole time I kept wondering if my team was winning. I had no idea what was about to happen.

"On lap twenty-eight through the neighborhood, my girlfriend finally told me she wanted to break up and go out every once in a while 'just as good friends.'

"I couldn't believe my ears. We had broken up before, but I had always initiated the breakup. This time she broke up with me and I was crushed, heartbroken.

"I didn't say a word and acted like it didn't bother me. I just kept walking until we reached her house again, where I told her to have my letter jacket and jerseys ready in the morning when I picked her up for school. I also told her she'd need to find a ride home for that afternoon. (Kind of rude, huh?)

"That week at school felt unbearable. When it ended, I left for the weekend to go to our family cabin. For two days, I cried. I was so miserable on the inside I thought I would die.

"I later learned that about a million teenagers go through the breakup of the century every year. One word best describes the experience: PAINFUL."

No matter which end you are on, breaking up is difficult. When you go through this, can you ease the pain? Yes! Ephesians 4:31,32 speaks to both people breaking up:

> Let all bitterness and wrath and anger and clamor and slander be put away from you, along with all malice. And be kind to one another, tender-hearted, forgiving each other, just as God in Christ also has forgiven you.

LOWERING THE BOOM

The "typical" breakup goes like this:

The pizazz is gone. One day you wake up, turn over and look at the picture of your sweetheart. In the past, looking at that picture gave you a charge, but this morning there is no charge, no excitement, no pizazz. You wonder why you are so madly in love.

You begin a full scale investigation of your sweetheart, checking out every action and every word. You notice the zit above his lip, the wart on his nose, and you conclude that your sweetheart isn't as great as you thought.

The grass is greener on the other side. Since you decided that your sweetheart isn't that great any more, you begin looking around. You notice some others you hadn't paid attention to before and develop an attraction fast. The grass is definitely greener on the other side.

You lower the boom. You decide you don't want to go together anymore, so you lower the boom. The way you express it goes something like this: "You are so special [translation: I've gotten to know you and I think you're a loser] and I have really enjoyed dating you [translation: I've been bored to death lately when we are together], but I think it would be best if we dated other people [translation: There are half a dozen people out there I would rather go out with]."

HEARTBREAK CITY

Regardless of how you word it, the other person usually hears the translation. So the typical breakup, especially among non-Christians, results in:

Bitterness. She feels badly hurt, like you led her on and let her down. These feelings turn into bitterness and she resents you for breaking up. She feels so hurt she won't forgive you, and after she dumps her Coke on your head, you can't forgive her either. Bitterness leads to all of the other problems.

Wrath and anger. She gets angry because you have hurt her. She lets you know about every fault you have. Soon you tune each other out, and you can no longer communicate. The next day she hands back your picture poked full of holes (from the darts). Your letter jacket comes back with the arms cut off, and your football jersey has been dyed pink.

Clamor. You shout and scream. The madder you are, the louder you yell. Your stuff is ruined. You've heard all of your faults. You can't control yourself any longer. You begin to bang her head against the locker while she scratches your eyes out.

Slander. She spreads rumors about you at school, enlisting all of her friends to help. No one sits beside you anymore. They won't talk to you. And they only look at you to sneer and whisper to each other.

Malice. You want to retaliate, so you form a hate club and get all your friends to join it. Together, you make twenty posters saying what a loser she is, and hang them all through the school.

THE BLOODLESS ALTERNATIVE

Breaking up is never easy, but it doesn't have to be a bloodbath. These suggestions will help you handle it correctly.

Be kind and tenderhearted. Every aspect of your dating relationship should be based on Ephesians 4:31,32, especially when breaking up. The bottom line is concern for the other person.

Don't break up until you have settled down. If you are angry, wait until that has subsided and you have confessed your anger to God and asked for His love.

Realize the potential hurt that breaking up can cause the other person. It can make him or her feel rejected or "not good enough," no matter how gentle you are. Think through how the other person may respond. Then do all you can to avoid adding to the pain.

Determine whether or not to break up. In some situations breaking up is a necessity. In the cases below, you should definitely break up:

- you realize your date is a loser (see chapter 3).
- you realize your date is a non-Christian (see chapter 4).
- you are distracted in your commitment to Christ (see chapter 10).
- your parents are opposed to you going together (see chapter 10).
- you are involved in physical impurity (see chapter 12).

Other times, you may want to break up, but for the wrong reasons. For example, your sweetheart may hurt you and you want to break up to get even. Or you may have problems getting along. In these cases you need to work on your differences and not try to get even or run away.

Ask God's guidance. Ask the Lord to give you wisdom and guidance in the best way to go about breaking up. He will help you not only with the right words, but also with the right attitudes. Pray for the other person, asking God to prepare that person's heart for the announcement.

Get some advice. Ask an older, more mature Christian (your parents, youth minister, or a Christian friend) if you are headed in the right direction. Be open to suggestions. Often this person will see things you don't see since he is not emotionally involved.

Think through your words. Before breaking up, think about what you are going to say and how you are going to say it. You do not want to "dump on God" — putting all the responsibility on God for the breakup. For example, you would not say, "God is telling me to break up with you." That's a cop-out! You must be tender, but also straightforward and honest. Give the specific reasons you think it is best to break up.

If you break up because the person is not a Christian or because they don't pass the test in chapter 3, then let the person know that. Stress the fact that your relationship to Jesus Christ has to be the most important aspect of any relationship. Explain that continuing to date would not encourage that. Steer clear of a "holier than thou" attitude, but be honest.

If you are breaking up because of physical compromise, ask for forgiveness first. Then explain that you need to break up while you grow strong in that area. Add that continuing to go together would be too risky until the problem is dealt with.

If you are breaking up because you realize "the other person is not the one," be honest — but again be kind and tenderhearted. First let him know the qualities about him that you do admire and appreciate. This helps soften the blow.

Talk in person. Show the respect you have for the other person by breaking up face-to-face. Do not break up over the phone or by letter. When you get together, go to an unromantic place, like a park during the day. Otherwise, you may be tempted to comfort the other person by showing affection. Many times couples have made up while breaking up only to have to break up again shortly afterward. That's called double pain!

Accept your responsibility for the breakup. When you talk, own up to any of the things you have done that kept the relationship from working out. Tell him that you are interested not only in your own benefit, but also in his. Breaking up is not a time to air grievances. Work those out ahead of time. However, during a breakup you must give reasons why you no longer believe you should go together.

Don't get talked out of it. Once you express yourself about breaking up, often the other person will try to talk you out of it. Watch out for these tactics to postpone the breakup:

- making you feel guilty
- intimidating you through anger
- playing on your mercy by crying or promising to be different
- being romantic with the hope of igniting the fires once again

Whatever the tactic, if you believe you are supposed to break up, then stick to your guns. Trust the Lord Jesus to take care of the other person's needs. You follow through on what you believe the Lord has led you to do.

Give the relationship time. If he says that he is different now or that he has changed, give him time to prove himself. This protects you from getting back into the same situation. Do this even if he says he has become a Christian. Getting back together too soon can divert his attention from his walk with Christ. If you want what's best for him, you will wait.

Don't put it off. When you know breaking up is the right thing to do, do it! Don't hang on out of obligation or in hope that he or she may change. The longer you wait, the harder it gets. The quicker you do it, the sooner you can learn what Christ has for you next.

Putting these guidelines into action do not make breaking up any easier, but they do help you follow through on what is right. Breaking up usually brings pain. But following this route will let the other person know that you want what's best for both of you.

WHY ME?

Now put the shoe on the other foot. Let's look at how to deal with it when someone breaks up with you. As wonderful as you are, someone sometime may make the grievous mistake of ending a dating relationship with you. Here are some reasons your steady may give to explain the breakup:

Someone "better" came along. The relationship seems to be moving along nicely. Never before have you enjoyed each other so much. Then it happens. A new guy or girl comes on the scene. It may be someone completely new to the campus, or just someone your steady hasn't noticed before. Not long afterward you find yourself listening to the words, "I think it's time we started dating other people."

The tendency is to think you have been replaced by someone better. Replaced, yes, but don't think this new person is better than you. Just different. God made you a very special person. Because your steady starts to date someone different doesn't make you a loser. Your dating status is all that has changed, not your specialness.

You don't want to "mess around" physically. Many couples break up because one of them wants to mess around and the other doesn't. This may not be the reason given to you, but you know it is true nevertheless.

Ladies, to handle this, suggest that your boyfriend first ask your father if he can marry you. It's amazing how guys will tell you they love you but do not want any of the responsibility that goes with it. Girls, too, can want the thrill without any obligation. So, men, tell her to get signed permission from her parents first.

Things just didn't work out. Although this is the easiest reason to accept, it is still painful. Many times steady relationships are not meant to last. While going together you discover that you are not meant for each other. One of you would have needed to initiate the breakup sooner or later. It just so happens that it was the other person. To find out as quickly as possible that the relationship is not right keeps one of you from being led on.

IT HURTS SO BAD

Perhaps painful is not the word for it. Breaking up is emotionally tearing. You probably identify with some of these hurts.

Confusion. Many times a breakup causes confusion. You don't understand why it is happening. You had no idea until you found yourself talking about it. You may have thought you had found the person you wanted to marry but now you aren't even going together anymore. You have tried and tried to figure it out, but nothing makes sense.

Loneliness. Before, you were always with your steady. Now you are alone. It feels like something (someone) is missing. You no longer have that special person to talk to who understands your deepest thoughts and feelings.

Low self-image. You feel rejected. This always hurts, especially when someone whom you care for deeply hurts you. You feel that if they don't want you, then nobody else will either. You feel unimportant. It's hard to imagine anyone ever liking you again.

Depression. You get so down in the dumps that you become depressed. Nothing seems to matter anymore. You don't feel like doing anything.

Fear. You decide "I won't get burned again!" So you tell yourself you will never date again. That's because you are reluctant to get yourself back in the same situation. If you got hurt once, why get hurt again? You may even like someone but the fear of being hurt again keeps you from asking that person out.

These are only a few of the ways you experience the pain of breaking up. How can you handle these feelings?

THE RIGHT RESPONSE

If you date, you always run the risk of rejection. And if

you commit to dating one person, you run an even bigger risk. So it makes sense to know how to respond if that happens. Most people think of only one type of response, the outward — what you do and say. But there are two other responses that you must make before you give an outward response.

1. *Your upward response.* When you realize your steady wants to break up with you (lowering the boom smack on top of your head), the first thing to do is pray. In the midst of the situation you may have to pray quickly, but you need to ask for the grace and strength to respond correctly.

2. *Your inner response.* As you go through the experience, ask Jesus to teach you everything He wants you to learn. Tune in your mind to pick up everything, because the tendency is to turn your ears off, start humming and think "Who is this total loser to say anything about me?" So remember that the Lord may want to show you things in your personality that need to be changed. Or He may use the breakup to identify ways you can relate better to the opposite sex in the future. You need to be open to learning everything you can. Now you are ready for your outward response.

3. *Your outward response.* How do you respond as the news breaks? The natural response: Break a vase over his head, call him names and stomp off. But the last part of Ephesians 4:32 tells you what your response should be: Forgive him just as God has forgiven you. Consider how many times you have hurt the Lord and how just as many times He has forgiven you.

After your steady has finished speaking:

- thank him for his honesty
- express appreciation for the special time you had together
- let him know how grateful you are for your friendship and assure him of your continued friendship.

YOU THOUGHT THAT WAS HARD?

If you thought responding properly was hard during the breakup, it can be even harder for the next three or four weeks after the breakup. How do you handle it?

Change your focus. For several weeks (or several years) you have focused on your sweetheart. Thinking and talking about him or her will trigger strong emotions. At that point, focus your attention somewhere else. The easy way out is to focus on another person right away. Avoid that. Instead, put your focus on the Lord. See this as an opportunity to grow closer to Jesus Christ. Ask Him to fill the void. Be honest with Him, and let Him deal with all those hurts. Ask Him to meet the needs your steady once met. This is the only way to fully recover.

Stay busy. This will help keep your mind off your old sweetheart. Fill up all your extra time you now have with projects like those found in chapter 8. Spend time with your old friends. Look for ways to make new friends.

Make needed changes. If you learned something about yourself that helped contribute to the breakup, begin to work on that.

Talk to a friend. If you continue having a hard time getting over the breakup, talk to your parents or to an older, more mature Christian. Don't go to several people, though, because that can be an excuse for wanting people to pity you or a plot to enlist others to help you get your old sweetheart back.

Avoid another close relationship. Often, to fill what's missing you look for another close relationship — quickly. That's not wise. Going from one relationship to another doesn't give you time to get your life under control. You need to be content without a relationship before you are ready for a new one. You need time for your emotions to heal. Failure to do this makes you a prime candidate for getting involved on the rebound and getting hurt again.

Continue your friendship. Don't see too much of your former sweetheart at first. Sometimes just the sight of him or the mention of his name causes you to lose control. But as quickly as you can, continue the relationship as friends. If you can't trust your motives, wait until you can. To wait a little longer and develop a true friendship far surpasses subtly trying to get him back.

TO END RIGHT, START RIGHT

Jesus Christ wants all your relationships to be positive, even when you break up. The best way for that to happen is to date the way Christ wants you to date from the beginning.

ACTION SECTION

1. If you feel like you are supposed to break up:
Write out why you should break up. _____
_____
_____

When you prayed about it, what did God show you? _____
_____
_____

Talk it over with a more mature Christian. What did that person say? _____
_____
_____

Write what you will say when you break up. _____
_____
_____

Write the results of your breakup encounter. _____
_____
_____

2. If someone breaks up with you:
Write how you feel. _____
_____
_____

Check here when your attitude is one of kindness and tenderness and not bitterness or anger. _____
Describe how you will use this as an opportunity to grow closer to Christ. _____
_____
_____

Write how you will fill up your time to stay busy.
This Friday night _____
This Saturday night _____
Long-term _____
What have you learned about yourself that you need to work on specifically? _____
_____
What one step will you take to work on this? _____
_____

3. Memorize Ephesians 4:32.

12

Setting Standards ♥

WHAT will your marriage be like? Perfect? Livable? Barely endurable? Broken? You can choose, because the choices you make today greatly determine whether your marriage will work tomorrow.

Those right choices are hard to make, especially with all the pressure to make the wrong choices. That pressure comes at you like this:

If it feels good, do it.

Do your own thing.

Why wait till marriage?

Live together.

Have an affair.

Take the pill.

Just get an abortion.

Porno — what's the hassle?

Homosexual? Lesbian? Bisexual? Whatever turns you on.

Everybody's doing it.
Just so it's meaningful.
As long as nobody gets hurt.
You've come a long way, Baby.
This is the new morality.
C'mon out of the Dark Ages.
Come out of the closet.
Get rid of those hang-ups.
Express yourself.
If you love me, you'll let me.
Don't repress it.
Go natural.
Get with it.
Be liberated.
Be free.
Let go.
Live![1]

And these are just a few! Do they sound familiar? It's tough to make the right choices when people are pressuring you to think like this.

What are the right choices and how can you make them in spite of the pressure to compromise?

NAIL IT DOWN

Have you ever "blown it" in a dating relationship? How often have you done something you thought you would never do? In order to avoid that again, you must make the right choices ahead of time. Dating standards help you do this. A dating standard is a choice about dating based on the Bible, that you put into practice. It is a choice that you will not compromise regardless of the consequences. Check out some ways standards will help you.

Standards keep you from slipping. We recently counseled five couples who got pregnant before they were married. None of them planned to get into trouble. They started their relationship innocently enough. As the weeks went by, the pattern progressed from holding hands to superholding hands. Later it was kissing to superkissing. Then it was messing around to supermessing around. Finally it was trouble to supertrouble. If they had set firm standards, they not only would have known where to stop, but more importantly they also would have stopped.

Standards protect you from high-pressure situations. While most students ease into compromise, some find themselves caught unexpectedly in a sudden, "Let's go all the way" scene. Having standards gives the strength to say no, because standards draw the line beyond which you will not go.

Standards guard you from making emotional decisions. Emotions deceive. They can carry you away. Without standards, you will make decisions based on emotional impulses. One look at those beautiful eyes could melt your heart. Standards keep you from living by your emotions.

Standards allow you to make decisions now. Waiting until you get in the middle of a tough situation to make a decision can get you in trouble. You may think you know what you will do, but you can never be sure. Those who wait to decide usually decide incorrectly. There's no time — or desire — to pray, study Scripture and seek the counsel of a more mature Christian. Standards allow you to make your decisions now while your thinking is clear, your feelings are under control, and your desire is for God's best.

Standards help you consider what is important. Most people tend to focus on the physical and the immediate. Rarely does someone concentrate on inner qualities or long-term results. For example, the couples we counseled focused on feeling good for a short period of time and completely ignored the long-term effects of having sex (like making babies). Standards point you to these considerations. They make you stop and look at what is important.

Standards discourage compromise in other areas. Compromise is contagious. Once you allow an opening in one area of your life, you will soon find compromise in other areas. Standards help keep that from happening.

Standards enable you to walk closer to Christ. Christ said that the gate is narrow and the way hard that leads to life (see Matthew 7:13,14). Standards serve as guardrails to keep you on the narrow path. Many students have fallen in the ditch on the side of the road because of improper dating practices. Standards keep you from falling in a ditch. They keep you in the center of the road.

THE CONSEQUENCES

Think about a time when you messed up by doing something you knew was wrong. How did you feel? What damage did you suffer? Four major areas in your life become dull when you compromise your standards.

Your worship. God loves you very much and wants you to love Him in return. When you worship God, you communicate to God your love for Him. The only thing that damages this worship is sin. Isaiah 59:2 says that "your sins have hidden His face from you." To God sin is the same thing bad breath is to you — it stinks. Anytime you sin God doesn't like the smell. He must hide His face. God still loves you but your sins hinder your worship of Him.

Your self-worth. When you do something wrong, you feel guilty. Even though you may try to excuse it, you know you are wrong. That can make you feel like God doesn't love you and that you are worthless. Fears and insecurities may creep in. Negative thoughts lead to more thoughts. Some people have gone so far as to convince themselves that there is no hope for them and they commit suicide.

Your witness. Few areas can discredit your Christian witness quicker than compromise in your dating. No one is fooled when you talk one way during the week and act another way over the weekend. Word soon gets around that you are a hypocrite. When you talk to someone about a personal relationship to Jesus Christ, he gets turned off. He thinks, "Who is this guy to tell me how to live?"

Your wedding. One of the greatest moments in life is

the day you get married. When Bill and Debby were married, she gave him a box with an old-fashioned key in it. Attached to it was a note:

Herein represents the key to my heart. I have never given it to another. Today, I gladly give it to you. How comforting to know it will never be broken.

When Bill read it, he was excited. His sweetheart had saved herself for him. Without standards, you cannot enter into marriage with this type of special commitment.

GOD'S BEST

To avoid these consequences and enjoy God's best for you — set standards. Romans 12:1,2 shows how to do this:

I urge you, therefore, brethren, by the mercies of God, to present your bodies a living and holy sacrifice, acceptable to God, which is your spiritual service of worship.
And do not be conformed to this world, but be transformed by the renewing of your mind, that you may prove what the will of God is, that which is good and acceptable and perfect.

These practical steps from Romans 12 will help you as you think about setting your own personal dating standards.

Step 1: Dedicate yourself to Jesus Christ totally. Your dedication is like a "living and holy sacrifice acceptable to God" (Romans 12:1). "Acceptable" means well-pleasing. You are well-pleasing to God when you keep yourself from compromise by following the lordship of Christ.

If you have never totally committed yourself to Jesus Christ, it's useless to set standards. It makes as much sense as someone bailing water out of a sinking boat instead of repairing the leak. Stop the leak first, then do the bailing. The same is true with standards. Once you totally dedicate yourself to Jesus Christ, then you can work on the specifics, like dating.

To commit yourself totally to Jesus Christ, pray this prayer of dedication right now:

Lord Jesus, I admit that I've been running my dating life. Please forgive me. Take control of my life right now. I will obey everything you show me to do. In Jesus' name, Amen.

Step 2: Determine your specific needs or struggles. When Romans 12:1 says "present your bodies," the word "body" means more than the physical body. It includes your mind, emotions, habits, and attitudes.

Different people struggle with different things. You may need standards on the kind of person you will date. Another may need to nail down how far is too far. Someone else may need to decide when to say "I love you." Whatever you need, you have to set standards to reach your goal.

Step 3: Discover God's perspective. After you determine your dating needs, then look in the Bible and see what God has to say about it. For example, if you need a standard about dating unbelievers, read 2 Corinthians 6:14-18. Study that until you know what Jesus Christ wants for you. If you don't know where to look or don't understand what a verse means, ask your parents, youth worker or a mature Christian friend to help you find the answer.

Step 4: Decide on your specific standards. Once you know what the Bible says, then write down your standard. That helps you to remember it, leaves less room for compromise and will motivate you to follow it. Follow these helpful hints as you write.

● Brief. Write the standard in one short sentence.

● Personal. Use the pronoun "I" or "me." Don't use "A Christian should . . ." but "*I* will . . ."

● Specific. Make your standards clear and measurable. Be specific enough so others will know if you keep them or not. For example, don't write "I will date better people," but "I will date only growing Christians."

● Action-oriented. Tell what you will do, not what you will be. For example, not "I will be nicer to my parents," but "I will obey my parents' desires about who I date, where I go and when I have to come home."

● Scriptural. In parentheses at the end of each standard put a Scripture. For example, "I will obey my parents' desires about who I date, where I go, and when I should come home (Colossians 3:20)." Referring to Scripture reminds you that you are not doing this for yourself but to obey God.

● Realistic. Make every standard reachable. If not, you will soon become frustrated and throw them all away. For example, you could write, "I will not kiss someone longer than sixty seconds." The problem: No one is going to keep time. A realistic standard would say, "I will not kiss lying down."

● Parents. Once you set your standards, go over them with your parents. This provides a perspective from someone older and wiser. They love you and have your best interests at heart. Also, this positive communication builds a closer relationship with your parents.

Step 5: Diligently practice. Romans 12:2 says "prove what the will of God is," which means to put God's will into practice. Don't wait until next semester. Start putting your new standards into practice now. If you are presently dating someone, communicate your standards and discuss any necessary changes in the relationship.

Step 6: Daily review. In Romans 12:2 you read, "Be transformed by the renewing of your minds." Your mind is the battlefield. What goes on in your mind, comes out in your actions. If you want to change your dating actions or relationships, you must renew your mind by reviewing the Scriptures for each standard. Go over at least one standard and Scripture each day. Keep these standards constantly before you and they will become a natural part of your lifestyle.

Step 7: Discourage tempting situations. Romans 12:2 reads, "Do not be conformed to this world." If you know you are weak in an area, do not test yourself by trying to do what the "world" (friends, others at school) does. Think ahead. See what's coming, and do everything to avoid it. For example, if you struggle with lustful thoughts, avoid movies that show sex. Or if you have problems keeping your security in Christ, stay away from consistent and commitment dating.

Step 8: Desire to withstand suffering. Romans 12:2 says, "proving the will of God." The word "prove" means to test. Sometimes keeping your dating standards will be very painful. Compromising would be much easier. Be willing to suffer the hurt before compromising your standards and you will prove to yourself and others that God's ways are best. Even if you suffer now, like losing your boyfriend or girlfriend, keeping your standards is always better in the long run.

Step 9: Develop accountability. To help you follow through on your standards, find another person you trust, someone who loves you and wants God's best for you. Ask him to hold you accountable. Ask him to check up on you to see if you are keeping your standards. Be honest. Talk frequently about how you are doing. Having someone to report to each week will motivate you to keep your standards.

GET STARTED

To help you get started, look at these key areas of dating. Beside each one is a suggested Scripture to help begin your study. Study all of these, then write a standard for those five most important to you.

Area	Scripture	Standard
Age to date	1 Timothy 4:12	
Person to date	Galatians 5:19-23	
	Psalm 1:1-6	
Dating non-Christians	2 Corinthians 6:14-18	
Getting a date	1 Peter 3:3,4	
	Proverbs 3:5,6	
How to date	Romans 13:14	
How to wait	Proverbs 31:10-31	

How to treat my date	Philippians 2:3,4
When to go steady	1 Corinthians 7:35
How to break up	Ephesians 4:31,32
Girls calling guys	Proverbs 11:22
Dressing for dates	1 Timothy 2:9,10
Guarding my reputation	Proverbs 22:1
Respecting my parents	Colossians 3:20
	Ephesians 6:1,2
Quality of the	Psalm 34:3
relationship	Matthew 6:33
Saying no	Colossians 4:4-6
Where to go on dates	2 Corinthians 8:21
	Romans 14:13
Kissing on dates	1 Corinthians 10:31
Meaning of kiss	Romans 16:16
Physical limits	1 Corinthians 6:15-20
	1 Thessalonians 4:1-8
	Proverbs 6:27,28
	Matthew 5:27,28
Response to roaming	1 Corinthians 7:1
hands	1 Peter 2:11
Response to a girl's	Genesis 39:7-12
come-on	2 Timothy 2:22
Public display of	Ephesians 4:17-24
affection	
Emotional attachment	Proverbs 4:23
Saying "I love you"	1 Peter 1:22
Showing love	1 Corinthians 13:4-8
Waiting till marriage	Song of Solomon 2:16
Purpose for dating	Ephesians 4:1-3

IF YOU'VE BLOWN IT

Standards will help you for the future, but what do you do if you've blown it in the past? That's a good question — and there is good news. You don't have to live with the mistakes of the past. You can move on. Here's how.

Confess all sin to God. The Bible says "If we confess

our sins, He is faithful and righteous to forgive us our sins and to cleanse us from all unrighteousness" (1 John 1:9). Get everything out in the open before the Lord. Agree with Him that what you did was wrong.

Receive His forgiveness. The apostle Paul tells us "There is therefore now no condemnation for those who are in Christ Jesus" (Romans 8:1). If you confess your sins, God forgives you. You are pronounced "not guilty." Receive God's forgiveness now.

Make your relationships right with others. Jesus said, "If therefore you are presenting your offering at the altar, and there remember that your brother has something against you, leave your offering there before the altar, and go your way, first be reconciled to your brother, and then come and present your offering" (Matthew 5:23,24). If what you have done has offended someone else, ask that person to forgive you. When you get things right, then you can move on.

Start over. The apostle Paul talked specifically about not letting past mistakes keep you down. "But one thing I do: Forgetting what is behind and straining toward what is ahead, I press on toward the goal to win the prize for which God has called me heavenward in Christ Jesus" (Philippians 3:13,14, NIV). Get up and get going.

PUTTING IT ALL TOGETHER

God's style of dating isn't easy. But no doubt, it is and always will be the best! Take the important steps of preparing yourself to date a winner. Learn how to pick a winner. Look to date only growing Christians who evidence Christ-like qualities.

Guys, once you take these steps, take the ten steps to the door to get a date. When you go out, be creative. Stay out of the rut of movies and pizza. And work on developing the Christ-like inner qualities that will make you the kind of person women are genuinely attracted to.

Girls, remember the difference between being a flirt

and being a friend. Look your best on the inside as well as on the outside. And don't forget to pray before you give the guy an answer. If you aren't dating right now, don't worry about it. Use the time to become the best person you can. To get the best, you must be the best.

Regardless of whether you are a guy or a girl, if you want to go out with the same person more than once, put your date's needs first. Use good manners and express appreciation often.

When it comes to going together, let your guide be undistracted devotion to Christ. Never allow your date to become more important to you than your relationship to the Lord Jesus Christ. This means that you may need to break up with someone from time to time. If that's the case, be kind and tenderhearted, but follow through. If you are on the receiving end of a breakup, forgive the person if you get hurt in any way.

Finally, decide now how you want to respond later. Set standards in your dating that you refuse to compromise . . . regardless of the consequences. Do this and get in on the joys of dating God's way.

Dating — fun or confusing? Hopefully, after reading this book, you will apply the things you learned so the fun will be maximized and the confusion minimized. God bless you in your dating.

ACTION SECTION

1. In your opinion, what is the most important reason to have dating standards? _____

_____

_____

2. What consequences are you experiencing in your dating because of wrong choices? _____

_____

_____

3. Pick three areas from the list in this chapter and set dating standards following the steps given for "Get Started."

	Area	Scripture	Standard
(a)			
(b)			
(c)			

4. Memorize Romans 12:1,2.

Notes

Chapter 1
1. David C. Shultz, "How's Your Love Life?" Article. Source unknown.
2. Adapted from Mark Stephens, "A History of Dating," *Live Option,* Vol. 3, No. 2 (1983), pp.1,2.

Chapter 3
1. Adapted from Florence Littauer, *Personality Plus,* (Old Tappan, NJ: Fleming H. Revell Publishers, 1982).

Chapter 6
1. Melody Green, "Uncovering the Truth About Modesty," (Lindale, TX: Last Days Ministries, 1982).
2. Green, "Uncovering the Truth"
3. Barry Wood, *Questions Teenagers Ask About Dating and Sex,* (Old Tappan, NJ: Fleming H. Revell Publishers, 1981).

Chapter 9
1. Mark Stephens, "A History of Dating," *Live Option,* Vol. 3, No. 2, (1983), pp. 1,2.

Chapter 12
1. Larry Tomczak, *Straightforward: Why Wait Till Marriage?* (Plainfield, NJ: Logos International,1978), pp. 1,32.

Bibliography

Green, Melody. *Uncovering the Truth About Modesty.* Lindale: Pretty Good Printing, 1982.

Shultz, David C. "How's Your Love Life?" Source unknown.

Stephens, Mark. "A History of Dating." *Live Option,* Vol. 3, No. 2. San Bernardino: Campus Crusade for Christ, International (1983): 2-3.

Tomczak, Larry. *Straightforward: Why Wait Till Marriage?* Plainfield, NJ: Logos International, 1978.

Wood, Barry. *Questions Teenagers Ask About Dating and Sex.* Old Tappan, NJ: Revell Co., 1981.

Appendix A
One Verse Makes It Clear

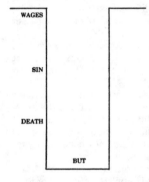

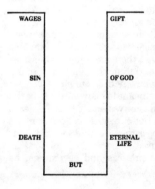

The story of the entire Bible, all 66 books, both Old and New Testament, is God's action to allow people to have an intimate, personal friendship with Himself.

One verse from the Bible and a simple diagram help make that clear.

In the New Testament, Romans 6:23 says, "For the wages of sin is death, but the gift of God is eternal life in Christ Jesus our Lord."

Now look how they fit into the diagram to make clear the concepts of sin, death, gift and eternal life.

Wages are the reward we receive for what we have done. How would you feel if your boss refused to pay you the wages that were due to you? We all know that it is only right that a person gets what he deserves. We earn wages from God for how we have lived our lives.

Sin is more an attitude than an action—it can be a hostile or apathetic response to God. At any point in your life, has God seemed far away? Our sin creates a distance between us and God.

Death often means separation—when we die our soul is separated from our body. If a person chooses to reject God while he is alive, that separation will extend into eternity; the separation will ultimately result in eternal torment in hell. Not only will he experience separation from God today, but also forever.

"But" is the most important word in the verse because it indicates that there is hope for all of us. God has good news!

A **gift** is not earned by the person who receives it, but someone else pays for it. Some people try to earn God's favor by doing good deeds, living moral lives, or taking part in religious activities. But it is impossible to earn something that has already been bought.

All of us have sinned, but **God** is perfect and

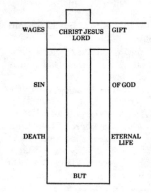

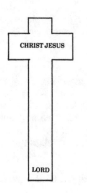

has not. God wants to give you a gift. A church can't give it to you; no one can give you this gift but God alone.

Eternal life means a relationship with God in blissful harmony forever. Just as separation from God starts in this life and extends into eternity, eternal life starts now and goes on forever. No sin can end it.

Jesus is the means by which we can obtain the gift of eternal life. No one can offer a gift except the one who purchased it. He purchased it by paying for it with His life.

Imagine that a police officer writes you a ticket for speeding and you go to court and the judge finds you guilty. But to your surprise, the policeman pays your fine out of his own pocket. In the same way, Jesus paid the fine—death—for you.

A person is dying because his heart is diseased. Someone volunteers to donate his heart for a transplant, knowing that he will have to die in order to give it up. But first, in order to save his own life, the recipient must agree to accept the heart. It cannot be forced upon him. In order to accept God's gift, you must make an important decision.

The gift is offered to everyone who makes Jesus Lord. For Jesus to be Lord, He has to have total control of a person's life. He gains that control, or becomes Lord, when a person does two things.

Confessing means to agree with God that we are not perfect, that there are things in our lives that are wrong, and that we want Christ to forgive us as we turn away from our sin.

To surrender means to allow Christ to be the final authority in our lives and to live in order to please Him and not ourselves. It doesn't mean that we have to be perfect, but that we will try our best to please Christ.

As a person confesses and surrenders, he

1. CONFESS

2. SURRENDER

1. CONFESS   2. SURRENDER

WAGES   JESUS CHRIST LORD   GIFT

SIN   OF GOD

DEATH   ETERNAL LIFE

BUT

passes across the bridge. He begins a relationship with God and starts to experience a new and eternal life.

If you were to place yourself on the bridge, where would you be? Are you far off to the left—far away from God—or close to the bridge and eager to learn more about God? Is there any reason why you should not confess and surrender right now and begin to experience a close relationship with God and receive eternal life?

If you would like to begin that relationship now, simply pray this prayer:

"Lord Jesus Christ, I need You. I agree with You that I am not perfect, that on my own I cannot earn Your gift of eternal life. I turn away from the sin in my life, and I surrender myself to You. I give You final authority in my life. I will try my very best to please You. Thank You for paying the price for my sin. In Jesus' name I pray. Amen."

WE'D LIKE TO LEAD YOU ON.

This book helps you replace society's misleading view of dating with God's exciting plan. Now we'd like to take you farther. At Breakaway, a one-day seminar on love, sex and dating. We'll make you laugh -- and think. Just like this book, which is based on Breakaway.

While you have fun, we'll show your youth leader a complete strategy for helping students accept Christ and grow in Him.

Just mail the coupon below for details on how Breakaway can lead you on. Without misleading you.

ReachOutMinistries

© 1987, Reach Out Ministries

Bill Jones and Barry St. Clair

Handle
Your
Hassles!

Let popular youth speaker Bill Jones guide you through meaningful, contemporary Bible studies that help you succeed in life! These four-lesson studies are available now:

- *PARENTS: Raising Them Properly*
- *SELF-IMAGE: Learning to Like Yourself*
- *PEER PRESSURE: Standing Up For What You Believe*
- *TEMPTATION: Avoiding the Big Rip-Off*

And watch for more "Handling Your Hassles" studies to be published soon by Here's Life Publishers!

Available at your
Christian bookstore

Or call

Here's Life Publishers

Toll free 1-800-854-5659
In California call (714) 886-7981

Planning a Retreat, Student Conference or Discipleship Weekend?
Then consider a

HANDLING YOUR HASSLES CONFERENCE

From the following topics, choose what would best meet the needs of your students.

PEER PRESSURE
How to stand up for what you believe

PARENTS
How to raise them properly

SELF IMAGE
How to like yourself

TEMPTATION
How to avoid the rip off

DATING
How to get a date

SEX
How far is too far

LONELINESS
How to make and keep friends

LOVE
How to spot the real thing

MARRIAGE
How to find Mr./Miss right

THOUGHTS
How to take the garbage out

For more information on scheduling one of our speakers, contact:

STUDENT MISSION IMPACT
Mobilizing Christians For World Evangelization

P.O. Box 2200
Stone Mountain, GA 30086
404-934-3831